This is an authorized facsimile
printed by microfilm/xerography on acid-free paper
in 1985 by
UNIVERSITY MICROFILMS INTERNATIONAL
Ann Arbor, Michigan, U.S.A.

THE INFALLIBILITY DEBATE

THE INFALLIBILITY DEBATE

Gregory
BAUM

George
LINDBECK

Richard
McBRIEN

Harry J.
McSORLEY

Edited by John J. Kirvan

PAULIST PRESS   NEW YORK N.Y. • PARAMUS N.J. • TORONTO

Acknowledgments

The article by Gregory Baum has previously appeared in *The Ecumenist*, Vol. 9, No. 3 (March-April, 1971) under the title "Truth in the Church —Küng, Rahner, and Beyond", © 1971 by Paulist Fathers, Inc. Printed by permission.

The article (Part I) by Harry J. McSorley has previously appeared in *Worship*, Vol. 45, No. 6 (June-July, 1971) under the title "A Response to Küng's Inquiry on Infallibility I", © 1971 by The Order of Saint Benedict, Inc. Printed by permission.

Published by Paulist Press
Editorial Office: 304 W. 58th St., N.Y., N.Y. 10019
Business Office: 400 Sette Drive, Paramus, N.J. 07652

Printed and bound in the
United States of America

The Infallibility Debate . . .
A Foreword

Growing around the edges of the infallibility debate is a suspicion that the whole affair is a pseudo event.

For some it smacks of a churchy quarrel, artificial and manageable, that is being given preference over the real issues that rack our times.

An extravagant diversion.

For others it is an inflated book-review exercise that somehow has escaped from the learned journals onto the pages of the news-weeklies.

For every breath of suspicion, however, there are two of disinterest. "So what!"

It is hard to gainsay this kind of response. For as long as the North American response remains as it stands, it is fully justified.

As long as it is an intrafamily argument about the truth or falsity of the doctrinal language of Vatican I, it does smack of "churchiness."

As long as the response is limited to carefully hedged reviews of the Küng book and the Rahner-Küng exchange, it does tend to rest within the category of book-reviewing.

Unless the perimeters of the debate are enlarged and unless the questions, the serious questions which it leads toward, are treated, then the debate stagnates and is, in truth, not worth continuing.

The theologians who have created the book which follows continue the debate precisely by enlarging the concern and pursuing the depths of the question.

It is the Lutheran, George Lindbeck, who reminds us most forcefully that if for Catholics the debate began with Hans Küng, it has been debatable in the larger Christian community for a long time.

In the other essays it becomes even clearer that the question can no longer be worked out in the narrow confines of the Catholic Christian community but must be seen within the breadth of Christianity.

The debate must go as deeply as looking at the possibility of Vatican I's action in the light of Vatican II's vision of the Church and its understanding of ecumenicity and councils.

The possibility and character of religious truth must be examined. And what are the terms of its formulation?

Not only must it be asked: What is the truthfulness of doctrine? It must also be asked: What is it supposed to mean?

What indeed is the relationship between the believing theologian and the community of his commitment? How does he function with relationship to defined doctrine?

Only when these questions and any others that are inseparably woven into the infallibility question are faced honestly and with some openness to the future, is the current debate worthy of more than a cursory review or an inevitable lack of interest.

The men who write here deal with the Rahner-Küng exchange. They go on, however, to the other questions. There are no settlements here but an attempt to expand the question to the size where it deserves a continued wide interest.

John J. Kirvan, C.S.P.

Gregory
BAUM

*H*ans Küng's new book *Infallible? An Inquiry* [1] raises the question of truth in the Church. He denies, at least provisionally, the Catholic doctrine of ecclesiastical and papal infallibility. Yet, the discussion stirred up by Hans Küng's book is not exclusively of Catholic interest. The question of truth preoccupies every Christian Church. All Christian Churches affirm, in one way or another, that the Church abides in God's truth. They all hold that the Gospel of Christ is available in the Churches to those who seek it. At the same time, they are willing to acknowledge that they have been short-sighted in the past and confused in the present, and that at times this lack of insight has led them into error. How can we combine the Church's claim to remain faithful to God's Word with the doctrinal errors she has made? Even the Churches, eager to concede that they have committed many errors in the past, do not consider erroneous the Gospel-faith on which they stand. The critical confessions of their own errors are based on the profound conviction of being rooted in the truth. Küng's book, therefore, touches issues of universal importance in the Christian Church.

In this article, I wish to examine what we mean by Christian truth. I shall begin by presenting Küng's own thought in his recent book, then analyze the eager refutation of Küng's position by Karl Rahner, and finally, by comparing and contrasting their views, indicate the direction in which, according

1

to my view, the solution of the problem will be found. I hope
to show that we are in need of more extensive reflection of
what religious truth is.

Küng's Position Examined

Abiding Truth Despite Mistakes

Küng begins his study by concentrating on the doctrinal
errors of the Catholic Church. He presents a long list of doctrinal positions that have been changed in the Church's history
and supposes that in most of these doctrinal modifications it
was a question of correcting an erroneous position held in the
past. The examples most in the mind of Catholics today are
the doctrinal changes introduced by Vatican II. Most dramatic
among these is the conciliar teaching on religious liberty. After
the popes of the 19th century had vigorously rejected religious
liberty as a moral and civil right of persons and condemned
Catholic authors defending this liberty, Vatican II, following
considerable conflict on the Council floor, corrected the
Church's official position. Vatican II declared that religious
liberty is a strict right of the human person which a just constitution must protect and promote.

There were other corrections of former teaching. The
fundamentalist approach to the Scriptures, advocated by the
popes at the turn of the century and expressed in the condemnation of books and in other doctrinal decisions, was
finally overcome at Vatican II. After considerable conflict,
Vatican II recommended the use of the critico-historical
method in the study of the Scriptures. The Catholic Church's
changing attitude toward ecumenism was also startling. While
Pope Pius XI still condemned the ecumenical movement and
was unable to acknowledge the common ecumenical bond created by baptism, Vatican II regarded the ecumenical movement as a gift of the Spirit, urged Catholics to participate in it,
and joyfully acknowledged the common Christian ground created among believers by baptism and many other gifts of

Christ. Also of special interest was the correction of a position to which Pope Pius XII had been greatly attached. In several encyclicals Pius XII had affirmed, against a wide theological tradition, that the Catholic Church was identical with the body of Christ and that Christians who did not belong to this Church could in no way belong to this body or be enlivened by the Holy Spirit. Pius XII forbade Catholic theologians to call this teaching into question. Vatican II happily corrected him. The Council modified the strict identity between Catholic Church and body of Christ, acknowledged ecclesial elements outside the Catholic Church, and, more than that, recognized other Churches as communities used by the Spirit to save and sanctify men.

For Hans Küng, Pope Paul VI's encyclical *Humanae Vitae* was a most significant error of the Catholic Church. Against the advice of his own study commission, Pope Paul confirmed the teaching of his predecessors that contraception was intrinsically evil and hence never permissible. Hans Küng thinks that Pope Paul went against the moral experience of contemporary men and the advice of the large commission of cardinals, bishops, theologians and specialists because of his deep conviction that the Church's moral teaching, universally preached by bishops all over the globe, was by this fact alone infallibly true and hence irreformable. While the majority of Catholic theologians do not have such a wide notion of infallibility, the Roman theologians have often made these excessive claims, and it may well be that Pope Paul followed them in this. Küng concludes that the colossal error of *Humanae Vitae* demands that the entire question of infallibility be raised.

Küng enters the problematic of truth in the Church by reflecting on the errors in her teachings. This, to my mind, is one-sided. While in his subsequent treatment Küng also deals with the much wider issue, namely, the historicity of truth, he does not sufficiently distinguish the two aspects and hence leaves himself open to the criticism of Karl Rahner and other theologians who have made this historicity a special object of study. After all, even if the Church had never made a single doctrinal error, it would still be necessary to reformulate and reinterpret her teaching as she moved from one cultural age to another. Küng deals with this historicity, but his main preoccupation is with errors, and this makes his perspective too narrow.

The Church has made doctrinal errors. At the same time, as a believer, Küng is firmly convinced that the Church is the bearer of the Good News. Guided by the Spirit she makes divine truth accessible to the world. How then does he combine the abiding truth of the Church with the errors she has made? He has a brilliant idea: he develops a very persuasive analogy to divine truth in the Scriptures.[2] The Church has always regarded the Bible as the Word of God and, as such, the privileged vehicle of the divine message. At one time Christians concluded from this that there were no errors in the Bible. When modern critical scholarship found a good many errors in Scripture, theologians tried in various ways to reconcile the divine truth with these errors. Some theologians distinguished in the Scriptures the inspired and the uninspired sections, and claimed inerrancy only for the former. This theory was not successful, for every time a biblical section was regarded as inspired and inerrant, the marks of human fallibility were also found in it. Thus, theologians came to the conclusion that the entire Bible was the Word of God and in all its sections communicated divine truth to the reader, despite the mistakes found in it. While this explanation at first shocked the Christian community and provoked the condemnation of bishops and popes, it eventually became the Church's official position. Despite mistakes, the Bible unfailingly communicates the truth of salvation to men.

In similar fashion, Küng suggests, critical scholarship has established many errors in ecclesiastical teaching. How do theologians handle this? At first they tried to distinguish between infallible and fallible teaching, and admitted errors only in the latter category. But this theory did not work. According to Küng, every time that the range of infallibility was defined, new research brought out the problematic character of some of the so-called infallible teaching. For this reason, then, why not affirm, in analogy to the truth in Scripture, that *despite the mistakes* the Church communicates the Gospel without fail? Küng calls this the indefectibility of the Church.

Whatever limitation this analogy may have, there is a good deal of truth in it. The important events that affect our lives are communicated to us in many conversations [3]—through stories, reports, messages, poems, songs, etc. If we know and trust the people who communicate these events and their meaning to us, we are quite sure that they hand on the significant truth, but we do not for a moment suppose that any one sentence in these conversations is infallible. As we examine the written record of these conversations more carefully, we may indeed find ambiguities, lack of precision, some faulty descriptions, a few misleading expressions, sometimes even outright error, but this would in no way call into doubt the truth of these events, expressed in these conversations in hundreds of different ways. The assurance that the message is true and important does not rest on the truth claim of any one sentence in these communications. Despite the mistakes, then, these conversations communicate the truth.

Karl Rahner's objection to Hans Küng, as we shall see, at first misunderstood the latter's position. Rahner interpreted Küng as saying that all of the Church's dogmas may be wrong. This is not Küng's position. The Church communicates the divine truth through Scripture and liturgy, through many words and gestures, among which the dogmas have a special place. To claim that this communication is indefectibly true does not mean, according to Küng, that any one sentence by itself can claim to be infallible. Future research may discover that this or that sentence is inadequate, possibly even wrong. Since divine communication is truthful, it is of course impossible that all the sentences employed in it be wrong. Küng simply affirms a sound principle that a truthful and powerful communication of important events does not depend on the infallibility of any single sentence in it. For the important things will be said in a hundred different ways, in many contexts, from many points of view: a few mistakes in no way weaken or invalidate the truth of the communication.

Here, as well as in other places in his book, Hans Küng is moving away from a highly conceptual understanding of truth to a more realistic description of what vital truth is. Unfortunately he never concentrates on this issue.

Three Kinds of Doctrinal Statements

Küng does raise the question, however, whether authoritative doctrinal pronouncements have a place in the Church's communication of the Gospel. In addition to Scripture, liturgy, preaching and Christian conversation, do we need ecclesiastical dogma? To my knowledge he is the first Catholic theologian in recent times to examine this question anew. To deal with it, he distinguishes three different kinds of doctrinal statements.[4]

First, there are *recapitulating* statements which summarize in a single sentence an aspect of the story of salvation. Already in the New Testament we find such doctrinal statements. They became part of the liturgy from the beginning. "Christ is Lord" is an example of such a creedal statement. This statement is not a proposition.[4a] It has a multiple, many-leveled significance. It sums up the story of salvation that Jesus lived, suffered, died on the cross, rose and was exalted on the right hand of the Father; more than that, it recalls that this man Jesus was the Christ, in fulfillment of the ancient divine promises. The creeds of the early Church, we note, were made up not of propositions, but of statements summing up and proclaiming the marvelous works of God. The Church, Küng holds, will always be in need of such declarations. However, since these declarations do not have a clearly defined content, but sum up a story of multiple meaning and power, variously understood according to the context of the Church and the spiritual needs of believers, it does not make sense to call them infallible. They are true, but they are not propositions. They are kerygma and doxology.

Second, there are *defensive* declarations that condemn a particular anti-Gospel movement within or outside the Church. These authoritative statements intend to defend the Christian truth in a concrete historical crisis. We find such statements already in the New Testament. For instance, the trend in the Church that regarded the Mosaic Law as obligatory for Christians was condemned by St. Paul and the apostles as irreconcilable with the Gospel. The ecclesiastical authorities retain the power, Küng holds, to protect the Gospel in a moment of crisis. In most situations, the authorities will defend the Gospel by teaching, argument and persuasion. Only at exceptional moments when the divinely revealed ground on which the Church stands is questioned or undermined will they formulate such a defensive declaration. Such a declaration is binding, according to Küng. To go against it would be to sever oneself from the believing community. But since a defensive statement is an expression of practical policy, opting for one orientation among two or several opposing trends, it is not an abstract proposition. At a later age, in fact, it may become clear that a more nuanced understanding of the situation would have permitted a course not clearly seen then and possibly a different formulation of the defensive statement; but at the moment of crisis, the choice was not between truth and error in the abstract, but between several concrete historical possibilities. When the Church chooses one of these trends as the best embodiment of her self-understanding, this is indeed a practical decision binding on her members at the time, but not a speculative judgment of infallible truth.

Third, there are *explicitating* statements that try to elucidate the meaning of the Gospel according to a particular school of theology or trend of Christian piety. Such pronouncements, Küng holds, are not essential to the Church's communication of the Gospel. Many Catholic doctrines, we realize, are precisely this. For instance, the explanations of Christ's eucharistic presence and the consequences of Christ's redemption for his mother Mary are explicitating pronouncements. Küng thinks that there is no need for the Church to engage herself on such issues. Explanation and explicitation belong to theology: they are inevitably multiple and variable. It is a mistake to claim that they can be infallible.

For Küng, then, the Church's indefectible communication

of the Gospel includes certain binding pronouncements, certain dogmas, but these proclaim the truth not in a propositional, uni-valued mode which might justify calling them infallible, but in various other modes, which Küng outlines but does not fully examine and describe.

When Karl Rahner, in a second reply to Küng, seeks to extend the common ground between them, he admits that practically speaking, in operational terms, his (Rahner's) view of authoritative dogma may not be different from Küng's at all. Küng does acknowledge, after all, that the Spirit is present in the Church's proclamation and defense of the Gospel, at least of its core. Even if Küng denies that this dogma is infallible, he admits that it is binding on the contemporaries, that it must be followed by later generations of Christians, including theologians, and that these theologians may deviate from it only if, thanks to new research and fresh insights, they can adopt a position more faithful to the core of the Gospel. Rahner, on a different doctrinal basis, comes to similar practical consequences. Yet he must disagree with Küng in principle.

But how does the Church determine the core of the Gospel? Küng does not address himself to this question. Since he begins his study by reflecting on the Church's errors and not, as he might have, on the historicity of truth, he is able to avoid the important question whether the core of the Gospel —that is, its central thrust, message and focus—remains always the same, or whether it is in part a function of the Church's salvational situation in history.

Vatican I Re-Examined

The question of error and, distinct from it, the historicity of truth also come into play in Küng's examination of Vatican I, held in 1870. This Council, as is well remembered, defined papal infallibility, and in this context also claimed the infallibility of the Church in her authoritative faith and dogma. Küng examines this teaching from two points of view. First he argues that the biblical and historical foundations for this teaching are lacking today. Modern scholarship has found that the passages from Scripture and tradition, cited at Vatican I in support of this teaching, do not in fact support this teaching at all. Unless new research is able to find historical support for the claim that Christ gave his Church the gift of infallibility, the theologian must ask himself if he may still accept this teaching or if, because of his deeper knowledge of the sources, he must confess that it is wrong.

But Küng also pursues another line of thought. Vatican I wanted to affirm the Church's trust in the power of the Spirit to keep her in God's truth. Yet the Council made this affirmation by using a model of truth that was widely accepted in modern Europe—namely, a highly rational model derived from Cartesian rationalism. Truth is available in clear and distinct ideas. Küng claims, on the basis of research done by Walter Kasper,[5] that pope, bishops and theologians at Vatican I, whether they favored or opposed papal infallibility, basically accepted this highly rational model of truth. Presupposing, then, that teaching the truth meant proposing clearly defined propositions, the Council's witness to the abiding truth in the Church almost unavoidably became the claim of ecclesiastical infallibility. Küng argues that, because of the highly rational model of truth, Vatican I did not see the problem of truth as we see it today.

Küng does not resolve the question whether he should, because of the inadequate historical basis, look upon Vatican I's definition of infallibility as erroneous, or whether, because of the special model of truth presupposed, he prefers to look upon this definition as true, but historically conditioned and in need of reinterpretation.[6] Since he leaves the second alternative open, he does not place himself as far away from Karl Rahner's view as the latter seems to think.

Despite the mistakes, the Church remains in God's truth. This is Küng's position. But how is the Church maintained in this truth? In part, as we have seen, through creedal statements summing up the story of salvation and through defensive statements excluding certain choices as going against the Gospel. But the main source of the Church's truth is the Bible.

Hans Küng does not deny that the Scriptures must also be studied as historical documents, that they also contain errors, and that they also utter the divine message with presuppositions and through concepts that are no longer our own. They, too, are in need of reinterpretation.

At the same time, Küng adopts very strong language to express the pre-eminent place of the Bible in the Church. He calls it the *norma normans non normata*. The Bible is the measure of truth, itself unmeasured, measuring all other statements of faith. This expression, taken from traditional Lutheran theology, has acquired considerable importance in recent ecumenical discussions in Germany. To assure Lutherans that the Catholic stress on tradition does not mean the addition of new truths of faith nor belittle the Bible as the one source of faith, many Catholic theologians have adopted this phrase. At moments of ecumenical fervor I have made use of the expression myself. It is, however, a most unfortunate phrase. It was originally a rhetorical overstatement, an expression of piety, a fervent claim to be independent of tradition. Yet the Bible, despite its pre-eminent position, is not the measure, itself unmeasured, measuring all other truth. This is not how the Bible is actually used in the Churches. Throughout their life and history the Churches actually have determined what the center of the Scriptures is, and they read the entire Scriptures in the light of this central message and concern. The Bible is never a book situated in empty space. It is always found in a Church that already exists, that has a doctrinal tradition, a certain liturgy, institutions of various kinds and a definite tie to a particular culture. While the Scriptures do exercise a normative function in the Churches, the use of such a rhetorical expression obscures the difficult problem of how the Churches have actually determined the center of the Gospel, in the light of which they understand the Scriptures and their entire past.

At certain places Hans Küng makes claims for the Scriptures that seem excessive to me. He wants to relativize the dogmas of the Church in respect to the abiding, unchanging norm of Jesus Christ as present to us in the New Testament.

But the New Testament itself is an historical document and hence in need of reinterpretation. At this point fruitful conversation between Küng and Rahner must continue.

Rahner's Reply

Historicity of Truth

Karl Rahner wrote a very sharp reply to Küng's new book in *Stimmen der Zeit*.[7] In it he not only tried to refute Küng's position as erroneous but also suggested that by his position Küng has excluded himself from an inner-Catholic conversation. Why did the great German theologian, who has done more than any man to renew Catholic theology in the 20th century, choose to express his disagreement with Küng in such sharp terms? It is my view that in this controversy two contrasting trends in Catholic theology confront one another very bluntly. We must hope that they remain in conversation. After Küng replied to Rahner in the same *Stimmen der Zeit*,[8] Rahner responded a second time.[9] This time he had mellowed considerably. While he still disagrees with Küng and does not see how Küng can defend his position as a Catholic theologian, he actually continues his conversation with Küng on an inner-Catholic basis and seeks to extend the common ground between them.

Before analyzing Rahner's response to Küng, let me explain the difference between the theological approaches these two men have adopted from the very beginning of their work. Küng and Rahner represent two contrasting currents in Catholic theology.[10] Both theologians affirm the need for the reform of Church life and the renewal of doctrine. Küng's tendency is to stress the biblical witness, to conceive of renewal in the Church as a biblical critique of present teaching and practice, and to advocate the closest possible conformity of the Church to the New Testament ideal. While Küng does not deny that later developments in the Church may have been necessary, good and useful, he regards these developments as purely human: they remain for him under the judgment of the biblical norm. Much of Küng's brilliant theological and historical research has brought out the problematic character of post-biblical developments in the Church and demonstrated how enlightening and powerful the biblical message remains in the present situation.

Karl Rahner also regards the Scriptures as a normative witness for the entire life of the Church, but he holds—and he is followed in this by a great number of contemporary theologians—that the significant post-biblical, doctrinal and institutional developments, while never wholly without sin or free of human failing, may nonetheless represent God's revelatory action in the Church. This divine action is God's ongoing self-communication to the Christian community, which enables the Church to interpret the Scriptures as God's Word addressed to her in the present and to adapt her institutional life to the needs of the Christian fellowship. Thus the Church is faithful to the divine message, once and for all revealed in Christ to the apostles, only as she continues to interpret it out of her present salvational situation. To reform the Church and renew her doctrine, therefore, it is not necessary to return to the biblical models of institutional life and linguistic expressions. What is important is to reinterpret the witness of Scripture and past tradition so that God's gift of himself as Word and Spirit be made available to people in institutions that embody their present self-understanding and in concepts drawn from their contemporary experience of reality.[11]

While Küng has always been concerned with honesty, truth and error in the Church, Rahner has been much more interested in the historicity of all truth. Rahner has brilliantly shown that a doctrinal statement, made at a particular moment in the Church's life, has built into it historical presuppositions and philosophical concepts, and that the Christian witness of such a statement is made available to us only as we understand the historical circumstances of its first formulation. For while presuppositions and conceptuality are the vessels of the witness of faith, they themselves need not be part of it, they do not oblige later generations, and they may be left behind not simply as outdated but even, possibly, as erroneous. What is important for the Church is to reaffirm in the present the Christian witness present in the doctrinal statement, and this can be done only in terms and concepts drawn from contemporary experience and based on presuppositions that are critically examined. If truth is historical, then the truth of a doctrine cannot be preserved simply by repeating it; to protect and promote the truth, the doctrine must again and again be reinterpreted in the Church's ongoing history. Rahner has never taught that dogmas are immutable in the Church. On the contrary, he has always taught that the only way to remain faithful to the Church's dogma is to reformulate and reconceptualize it in the present. Almost his entire theological work, vast as it is, has been dedicated to the faithful reinterpretation of dogma, self-identical with itself and yet new, powerful, relevant.

Hasty Argumentation

With this flexible approach to Church teaching, we might have expected Rahner to be more open to Küng's new book. Yet Rahner is angry with Küng since he detects in his book a lack of trust in the post-biblical developments in the Church. If we do not believe that the Spirit was at work in the Church during the past centuries, what reason do we have to suppose that the same Spirit is involved in the present crisis? Rahner is angry with Küng because he approaches the wide and complex problem of the historicity of dogma only by reflecting on the errors in Church teaching. Because of the anger, Rahner does not give Küng a fair chance. I think he misreads Küng, at least in his first response to him.

In his first response, Rahner makes two main points. First he tries to show that Küng is contradicting himself when he affirms that the Church remains in the truth and at the same denies that there are some infallible doctrinal statements. By a philosophical analysis Rahner tries to demonstrate that human consciousness determined by the truth is always able to express itself in some sentence that embodies this truth. This sentence is then as uncontrovertibly true as is the consciousness it expresses. He who remains in the truth, in other words, is capable of giving witness. The truth or falsity of this witness then decides the truth or falsity of the consciousness. Rahner concludes that Küng's position is self-contradictory.

This argument seems to me quite inadequate. I agree, of course, that the consciousness of the truth will always be able to express itself in some way using words and gestures, but there is no reason to suppose that this will always be in clearly defined statements. A man may feel that the truth of which he has laid hold cannot be adequately expressed in propositions. Jesus himself gave witness to the truth in parables. He told stories. In fact, the great men of religion have always preferred to give witness to the truth in symbolic language, capable of being interpreted on several levels—in a language, in other words, that continues to speak to us after it has been understood the first time. When Jesus was asked about the limits of fellowship, he told the story of the Good Samaritan. But for what sentence in this story do we want to claim infallibility? In his argument, Rahner reveals one of the limitations of the theological tradition, namely the highly rational understanding of truth.

Rahner's second argument against Küng is drawn from authority. Rahner claims that a theologian ceases to be a Catholic if he rejects a doctrine defined by a Council of the Church. He may remain a Christian theologian, but he argues out of a set of presuppositions that is no longer Catholic. By rejecting Vatican I's definition of infallibility, Küng has excluded himself from the inner-Catholic conversation.

This argument does not reflect the much more nuanced position taken by Rahner in his studies on the historicity of truth. There Rahner recognizes that the Scriptures and, in a different way, conciliar documents are divinely guided and at the same time remain human documents. As human documents they include presuppositions and models of thought that are peculiar to a particular age. If the theologian specifies these presuppositions and models and proves that they are no longer acceptable today, then he may, without being unfaithful to Scripture or council, separate himself from the literal meaning of the text—i.e., deny that it is literally true today—and interpret the divine truth present in this text in the light of the Church's present experience and in terms drawn from a contemporary intellectual tradition. Rahner admits that a theologian may very well disagree with the literal meaning of a conciliar definition. We recall that Küng himself has left open the question whether he should, because of lack of historical evidence, regard Vatican I as erroneous or whether he prefers, because of the model of truth employed at that Council, to reinterpret the Christian witness contained in it in the light of new insights and a more contemporary model of religious truth. If Küng opts for the second alternative, he finds himself very close to Rahner.

In his second, mellower response, Rahner recognizes the possibility that Küng may be quite close to him. Rahner admits that dogmas may become "erroneous"; by this he means that the questions to which these dogmas replied and the conceptuality in which they were formulated may change, and that by repeating these dogmas in literal fashion at a later time, we may in fact be saying something the dogmas never intended, something that has little to do with the Gospel, something that is wrong. The task of the theologian, Rahner repeats, is precisely to reinterpret the original dogma so that the divine truth proclaimed in it (not its literal meaning) can be uttered in the contemporary Church where other crucial questions have arisen and where other concepts are used to understand reality. Rahner insists against Küng that however inadequate, conditioned, problematic, and ambiguous the original formulation· of the dogma may have been, it was true. The dogmas defined by the Councils were true.

Yet even in his mellower response Rahner does not examine the more difficult question raised by Küng. What is the theologian studying conciliar documents to do when he finds that, because of recent scholarship, the historical basis for a defined doctrine has become problematic? The Council fathers in their age honestly took the biblical and patristic passages at their face value. They had good reason for defining the doctrine as they did. They had, moreover, the rightful authority to demand the loyalty of the entire Church. But what happens if modern scholarship finds that these passages had a different meaning? Rahner does not deal with this question. For him, the Catholic theologian begins by acknowledging the whole Catholic system and tries to reinterpret it in the light of the Church's contemporary faith. He leaves the historical foundation of this system to the study of fundamental theology. The great German theologian cannot be quite serious at this point! When reflecting and writing at peace Rahner will eventually recognize that the systematic theologian cannot shift the burden of this question on anyone else. The fundamental theologian, after all, cannot deal with this problem unless he employs concepts such as continuity and self-identity, taken from systematic theology. The question raised by Küng is a serious one and deserves the attention of systematic theologians.

It seems to me that even in his mellower response, Rahner retains a highly conceptual understanding of religious truth. He does not seem to realize at this point that the Gospel is handed on in the Church by a multi-leveled process, including words and actions, in which authoritative doctrinal statements have a certain role, but may never be identified with the Church's transmission of divine revelation. This transmission takes place through Scripture, liturgy, preaching, and many institutions and customs. It is usually called *traditio vitalis*, vital tradition.[12] The doctrinal tradition has its place in this wider framework, but we grasp the meaning of doctrine only as we understand its function in the Church's vital transmission of herself. There is no reason to suppose, it seems to me, that the entire tradition becomes faulty or insecure because of the discovery that one of the doctrinal statements believed to be true turns out to be based on some misconceptions. The actual transmission of the truth is so much vaster than doctrine that one does not see how it can be invalidated or harmed by such a discovery.

Karl Rahner is not as open to Küng's new book as his own (Rahner's) principles might have permitted him to be.

It seems to me that at this point nobody knows the answer to the uncomfortable questions raised by Küng. I concede that it may be true that the Church mediates the Gospel indefectibly, as Küng holds, though none of her pronouncements taken singly can be called infallible. Yet what he does not adequately examine is how the Church determines the focal point of the Gospel, in the light of which she understands the whole of the Scriptures. Rahner is here the better guide. Rahner has always insisted that it is impossible to suppose the indefectible transmission of the Gospel without a very special gift of the Church. What is this gift? Küng acknowledges it. He calls it indefectibility. But he does not examine it. Rahner rightly insists that the Church's role in the proclamation of the Gospel is greater than Küng supposes. The Church defines the center of the Gospel for her age. In my review of Küng's book in *The Commonweal* [13] I have followed the Rahnerian approach in specifying how I differ from Küng: "While he makes dogma relative in regard to the abiding scriptural norm, I think it is theologically sounder and historically more correct to make dogma relative in regard to the Church's ongoing, authoritative self-definition."

At the same time Küng has raised important questions which must be faced. While I have never followed him in his tendency to return to the Scriptures as the abiding norm and to advocate ever greater conformity of the Church to the biblical model, he has in his last book raised questions regarding the very nature of Church teaching which I consider very important. He has pointed out that the notion of infallibility, as defined by Vatican I, was based on a highly rational, if not rationalistic concept of truth. He has proposed, moreover, that the original dogmatic declarations of the Church were not in propositional form (except grammatically): they were either abbreviated formulas summing up the story of salvation or defensive statements rejecting as un-Christian certain concrete historical trends. Küng has proposed a principle that would enable the Church to simplify her doctrinal tradition and make authoritative claims only for issues connected with the core or center of the Gospel. For these reasons it is necessary that Küng and Rahner remain in conversation. Theologians may have to go beyond the present position of Küng and Rahner to clarify the nature of religious truth.

Dogma as Symbolic Truth

In the following section I wish to reflect on the nature of religious truth. For too long we have been content to look upon religious truth-statements as we do upon truth-statements having to do with ordinary life situations. A statement is true if it corresponds to the reality before us; it is false if it does not thus correspond. We tended to look upon religious statements as propositions of clearly definable content, representing a supernatural or sacred reality. Unless Christians were very sophisticated, they tended spontaneously to adopt a correspondence-theory of truth in regard to the Church's doctrines: religious truth was the conceptual conformity of the mind to the supernatural reality distinct from the mind and objectively present to it. Christians spoke easily of the being of God, of his properties, his intellect and will, taking for granted that these referred to a divine reality, distinct from them and facing them as a supreme object. We liked to say that the Church's dogma was objective. Doctrine refers not to human states, conditions and possibilities, but to the true God living in and by himself.

The great theologians, needless to say, never adopted such a naïve correspondence-theory of truth in regard to religious statements. They always understood, each in his own way, that the divine pervaded all being and in particular was operative in the very act of knowledge by which men recognize the divine in their lives. Since God is the source of human life and the ground of his significant wisdom and action, these theologians never considered God a divine reality existing apart from and above man as the supreme object of his mind, and hence never applied a simple correspondence-theory of truth to religious statements.

St. Thomas, for instance, with his famous principle of

analogy, taught that every positive statement about God must at first be negated. God is so different that no human statement utters a positive truth about him. Only after this negation has been taken seriously may we reflect on the certain similarity between God and creatures, and on the strength of this make a positive statement about God, a statement which, despite greater dissimilarity, does communicate something true about God. According to the Thomistic vocabulary, religious truth is never univocal. Religious statements never have a one-to-one correspondence to the sacred reality: they apply to God, after the negation of their literal meaning, according to a certain analogy. God is an object of the mind, therefore, only according to a certain analogy.

While the Thomistic analogy was taught in seminaries and universities, it did not affect in a lasting manner the consciousness of preachers and their listeners, nor did it exert a strong influence on God-language in the Catholic Church. For Catholics the doctrine of God was all too often a conceptual replica of the divine being existing in and by himself. Even in the writings of St. Thomas the principle of analogy is often presupposed rather than applied so that a reader may study the doctrine of God, with its manifold distinctions and detailed accounts, without ever being reminded that this doctrine is true only analogously—in other words, that it would be more true to negate it than to affirm it in a univocal sense. The enormous seriousness with which doctrinal statements were taken in the Catholic Church and the endless energy spent in arguing about them may also have contributed to the idea that these statements offered a precise conceptual representation of the supernatural reality.

This trend was intensified by the rational and scientific mentality of modern times. We recall the complaint of Maurice Blondel at the turn of the 20th century that a certain supernatural positivism pervaded Catholic theology and that God was looked upon as the supreme being outside of and above human history, the supreme object of the human mind. Blondel rejected this trend as "extrinsicism". Hans Küng in his recent book, basing himself on new research, shows that as a result of this modern mentality religious truth came to be looked upon in the Catholic Church as clear and distinct ideas. The time has come to return to the old masters of theology and to study contemporary thought in order to gain a more profound understanding of what religious truth is.

In the same modern age, however, we also discover a counter-tendency among theologians. Many theologians, standing aloof from the dominant trend in the Church, reflected more carefully on God's immanence in the world. They became more aware that the divine pervades the universe, encompasses and grounds it, and that it is present in human life as matrix and destiny. While these theologians would use traditional language calling God creator and king of the universe, ruling human history from above, they did not forget that such language must be qualified by declarations that the true God is never simply beyond but also within people who acknowledge him. God and man are not two fully constituted subjects who enter into conversation. God is present in man's becoming man. God is graciously present in the human growth that makes man a free subject open to faith, hope and love. According to Christian revelation, God's gratuitous gift of himself is the deepest dimension of human history: he is the source of man's personal and social destiny. In Protestant theology since Hegel and in Catholic theology since Blondel, many theologians have come to look upon the divine as the deepest dimension of the world, hidden from human knowledge, operative in history, disclosing itself at certain revelatory moments and thus initiating man into a new consciousness about himself, his origin and his destiny. In this perspective, we note, religious truth deals with a hidden reality present in human life and the universe.

Karl Rahner's own theology, we may add, is sympathetic to the trend described in the above paragraph. The so-called transcendental shift in his theology (not unconnected with Blondel's impact on Catholic thought) makes him less interested in the objective content of truth than in the conditions and presuppositions in the knowing subject and thus would make him quite willing to understand Christian doctrine as revealing the deepest hidden reality present and operative in human life.

If religious truth reveals the hidden dimension of human life, then we may not think of it as propositions with clearly defined content, corresponding to a supernatural object. Why not? Because the deepest dimension of human life can never be completely objectified. It is woven into our very being. It is the ground on which we stand, the light through which we know what really counts, and the freedom that enables us to forget ourselves in love. Religious truth expresses how man is related to this deepest dimension of his life, which is the divine mystery that encompasses him. Religious truth is not propositional in terms of a correspondence-theory of truth. Religious truth is symbolic.

The word "symbol" has two distinct meanings. One meaning, the more common one, is quite weak. A symbol points away from itself to another reality. A symbol has no power by itself: it simply recalls to the mind another reality which it represents. In this context a symbol is not understood as intrinsically related to the reality it stands for and hence participating in its power, but rather as an extrinsic and arbitrary designation of this reality, based on some imaginative likeness. To call dogma symbol in this sense would mean that dogma is a vague, undefined, subjective, more or less poetic image of the divine mystery.

There is, however, another meaning of the word symbol, a powerful one this time, which is also traditional and which has, in modern times, assumed considerable importance in the social sciences and the study of religion. Here the symbol expresses what no concept can, namely the manner in which man defines the ultimate meaning of his life. Here the symbol is a reality of power. For the way in which meaning and purpose are woven into human life is not something incidental which is added in an idealistic mood to a fully constituted world, but is constitutive of the very world in which man lives. The symbol is therefore a crucial factor creative of the world, the culture, the society to which men belong.

It was in the social sciences that the new appreciation

of the symbolic has first been regained. Sociologists, from the last century on, clearly understood that culture and society are not givens: they are made, they are produced by people. For instance, in his famous book *The Protestant Ethic and the Spirit of Capitalism* Max Weber showed that a crucial factor in the creation of the modern, rationalized, democratic, technological and bureaucratic world was a special kind of interiority, a special way of defining man's relation to the absolute, and he tried to demonstrate that this special interiority was supplied by Calvinistic Christianity. Why is it, Weber asked, that when a factory owner promises a higher rate for piece work, the German or American worker will work harder, while the Spanish working man may work less—for by noon he will have enough money for the day? The difference here lies in the way people define the meaning of their lives. Whether Max Weber was right in connecting the modern work ethic with Protestant asceticism is not important in this context. What is important is that he, and a wide sociological tradition with him, recognized that human action is never simply behavior, but behavior plus meaning. Meaning is constitutive of the human world in which we live.

How can the meaning that goes into the creation of human life be expressed? The sociologists were convinced that the meaning by which people live and the values in terms of which they interpret and order their experience are never fully conscious to them. Men's relationship to meaning and values is so deeply woven into their very being that they can never become fully aware of them. Ever since we are little children, we are exposed to values, norms, meanings and purposes through our parents and the social institutions (including language) of which they are part, so that we assimilate a system of symbols long before we achieve the rational maturity to be critical and search for our own values. Even when we reach this stage of maturity, we are never empty subjects in search of new meaning, for woven into our personal, intellectual, and emotional structure are the meaning and values in which we participated as we grew up. We are able to re-educate ourselves, but our deep convictions or doubts about love, trust, fidelity, and the orientation to grow are so deeply tied into our personal being that it is only on these and through these that we modify our conscious purposes. Man's relationship to the deepest dimension of his life remains inevitably implicit; it can never be conceptualized; it can only be spoken of in symbols.

The symbol, then, expresses man's relationship to the ultimate in his life. The symbol makes this relationship more conscious and communicable, and thus intensifies man's involvement in it. The symbol is, therefore, a powerful factor by which cultures are created, perpetuated, and, more important still, transformed. For Max Weber profound social change can only take place through some kind of religious inspiration, for only religion has the power to redefine man's relationship to the ultimate and create the symbols by which people build a new society.

Let me add that it was not only sociology that regained for us the powerful concept of the symbol. Psychology too has become aware of the unfinished character of man. Man is still in the making, his culture as well as his personal being. A crucial role in this creation of life is played by the imagination. The symbols which fill the imagination determine the way in which people interpret their lives, react to it and thus create their future. While reason has, of course, an important function in the choices we make, reason does not determine our basic attitude to life or the relationship to the deepest dimension of our existence. Reason does not determine whether we are afraid of the new and sense its dangers, or whether we regard it as a challenge and opportunity; it does not determine whether we are exhausted by work or whether it is an occasion for self-expression; etc. It is by the symbols in the imagination that life acquires or loses meaning for us. While these symbols are subject to rational critique, they are never reducible to reason; they are entities of their own with power over human life. William Lynch, in his *Images of Hope,* has shown how the imagination is the source of man's hopes, his well-being and creativity, and in turn how a lack of symbols, or destructive symbols, may lead to despair and ultimately to insanity.

The symbol, we conclude, as the expression of man's relationship to the deepest dimension of reality, is a powerful factor in the creation of human life. To say, therefore, that religious truth or revealed dogma is symbolic does not suggest that it is a weak statement representing the divine in a certain vague, lofty and poetic way, but rather that it is a powerful expression of the divine as it enters into man's self-definition and the world he makes for himself.

Let me immediately apply these remarks to the Church's trinitarian doctrine of God. This dogma reveals God's gift of himself to man as Father, Son, and Spirit. This dogma gives expression to the deepest dimension of human life, namely that despite the evil that threatens man, there is ultimately no reason to be afraid of life, for the ground on which man stands and the destiny which is his are *for* man, are on his side, are gracious. It reveals that present in human life is a summons or word, not of man's own making, which calls him to self-knowledge and empowers him to move creatively into the future, and that operative in human life is a love, transcending human resources, that draws man into friendship and orients him toward universal reconciliation. In my books *Faith and Doctrine* and *Man Becoming* I have tried to present the whole of the Church's teaching as the revelation of man's relationship to the deepest dimension of human life. Even the christological dogma of the Church announces that the self-communication of God in his Word, operative in a hidden way in all people and conditionally and provisionally constitutive of their personhood, has become fully incarnate and visible, in an unconditional and definitive manner, in Jesus Christ. In him God graciously discloses who he is, and who we as men are.

Religious truth is symbolic. What consequences does this have for doctrinal truth in the Church? It is my opinion that the Küng-Rahner controversy will make Catholic theologians reflect more on the truth-status of Christian doctrine. Let me draw a few conclusions from the considerations made on the preceding pages.

First, if religious truth is symbolic, then it does not have one meaning, but has meaning on several levels. Since the deepest dimension of human life is forever unobjectifiable, doctrine continues to have new meaning even after it has been understood and assimilated. Doctrine continues to address man, unsettle him, make him see more clearly the hidden dimension of his life, and lead him to a new consciousness. In more traditional terms, doctrine gives witness to God's Word and thus becomes a medium through which God addresses himself to man.

Second, if doctrine is symbolic, then it reveals the meaning of life. It is never an abstract statement. It makes known to man the hidden mystery operative in his life, appointing him to a task, drawing him into reconciliation and friendship, and giving him a glorious destiny. Doctrine thus makes sense! It may happen that doctrines that made sense to people at one time, that tied into their lives and gave them meaning and power, have become abstract. Because man's problems and his self-understanding have changed, these doctrines are no longer symbolic. Can they then still be called true?

Third, doctrine transforms human life. Since religious truth expresses man's relationship to the divine present in his life, it makes men more conscious of who they are and enables them to participate more intensely in this divine mystery. We touch here a traditional theme: God revealed himself for man's salvation and Christian doctrine is, therefore, a means of salvation. Doctrine converts man. It communicates a truth that liberates man, protects. him against the self-destructive powers, initiates him into a new self-awareness, intensifies his self-possession, and ever reconstitutes him as the new man. In doctrine the *verum* and *bonum* are inseparably intertwined. Religious truth is salvational.

Doctrine is true, we conclude, if it gives expression to, and makes men more conscious of, the gracious relationship that links them to the deepest dimension of their lives, as disclosed in Jesus Christ.[14] Doctrine is, therefore, always related to the Scriptures. But since doctrine must make sense today, it is never simply the repetition of the biblical creeds. Doctrine must be formulated again and again.

Karl Rahner acknowledges the symbolic nature of religious truth. It is central to his thought.[15] He draws an important consequence from this, namely the Church's need to reinterpret her dogma in terms of man's contemporary experience of life. In his new book, Hans Küng also alludes to the symbolic nature of religious truth, but draws a different, though equally radical, conclusion from it. He wants to free the Church from the burden of a doctrinal heritage that has become irrelevant. Why can these two perspectives not be combined?

Hans Küng, we recall, held that the Church's authoritative pronouncements include two types of religious statements. First, there are recapitulating statements summing up the history of salvation. They express Israel's relationship to the divine presence in her life as a model for our own self-understanding, personal and social. Second, there are defensive statements excluding false symbolic interpretations of life, offered by certain movements existing in history. These two kinds of pronouncements are not doctrinal propositions; they are much wider and more concrete utterances of truth. They come very close to what we have called symbolic truth. The conceptual clarification of these symbols, however, in what Küng calls explicitating statements, is not an essential part of the Church's authoritative teaching. They communicate new ideas, not new consciousness. On the strength of this principle, it should be possible to simplify Christian teaching considerably.

Self-Identity and Reinterpretation

If doctrine is symbolic, if religious truth continues to address people, makes sense to them, and initiates them into new consciousness, then there is need for reinterpreting the Gospel as the Church moves into a new historical situation. We noted above that Karl Rahner has been much more conscious than Hans Küng of the need for doctrinal development. Küng, we recall, approached the problem of the Church's fidelity to truth mainly by concentrating on her doctrinal errors. Rahner, on the other hand, stressed the more central issue, namely the inevitable historicity of truth. Because of this historicity the Church can be faithful to her past teaching only by reinterpreting it in a new age.

It is generally true that every sentence that is actually spoken is part of a conversation. There is always someone who speaks and someone who is being addressed. Even when a man is alone in the room and thinks, he replies to questions he has posed to himself. Thinking is an inner conversation. The meaning of a sentence, therefore, can never be obtained by analyzing the terms used in abstraction from the historical situation in which the sentence was uttered. The speaker brings to the sentence his own history, his problems and concerns, and he replies to a partner who has formulated his spoken or unspoken questions out of his own experience of life. The true meaning of a sentence can only be determined if we insert it into the original conversation in which it was first formulated. This is one level of the historicity of truth.[16]

In the Church the essential conversation is about the Gospel. Christians ask themselves what the Gospel means to them, how they understand their own lives and the society to which they belong in terms of Jesus Christ, how they experience the Word of God addressed to them in the present, and what the Scriptures mean to them as they read them with their actual questions and problems in mind. The conversation in the Church is grounded in the Church's experience, in her actual involvement in history, in her life as a community. To find the meaning of a statement, therefore, we must not only insert it into the original conversation but also try to understand what role this conversation played in determining the Church's self-understanding. This is the second level of historicity characteristic of Christian truth.

If a sentence, uttered in an historical conversation in the Church, is inserted—centuries later—into another conversation in the Church, when the crucial problems and the concepts for understanding reality have changed, then this sentence will say something quite different. As the Church enters a new age, she cannot be faithful to her dogma simply by repeating it. In order to preserve and proclaim the Christian message she must again and again reinterpret her doctrine. The traditioning of the Gospel, in other words, is a creative process in which the Church responds anew to God's Word and formulates it as the divine message addressed to the age in which she lives. The source of faith in the Church is not Scripture alone, to be endlessly repeated, but Scripture and tradition, i.e., Scripture and the Church's new, Spirit-created response to God's Word addressing her in her own experience.

How can the Church reinterpret her dogma without changing the Gospel? How can we preserve the self-identity of God's self-revelation in Jesus Christ as we reformulate the symbols in which we proclaim it? Hans Küng does not deal with this question. He feels that by going back to Scripture as the abiding norm, the Church will be led into the truth. But the theologians who have dealt at length with the historicity of truth have insisted that the reinterpretation of doctrine is possible only because of God's ongoing self-communication in the Church today. Whether we read Rahner or Schillebeeckx or Leslie Dewart, we learn that the task of reinterpretation (or reconceptualization) cannot be achieved by a theologian who, standing aloof from his own and the Church's experience, wishes to analyze what the doctrine meant when it was first uttered and then, in purely scholarly fashion, tries to clothe this truth in contemporary language and derive from it implications for contemporary problems.[17] Faithful reinterpretation is never such an intellectual achievement. Doctrine cannot be distilled from its historical roots and then poured into new vessels. Doctrine, as we saw above, always expresses man's concrete, historical relationship to the divine present in history.

It is, therefore, only because God continues to communicate himself in his Word, self-identically with the Gospel once for all revealed in Christ, that the Church can trust her Spirit-created, Scripture-tested experience as the focal point, in the light of which she may reinterpret her past teaching. Rahner and Schillebeeckx prefer to speak of the new "horizon" in which the Church finds herself and in terms of which she must reinterpret her doctrine. Dewart speaks of the Church's present experience and consciousness. I have preferred to say that, thanks to the Church's faithful listening to God's Word addressed to her in the present, she is able to discern the focal point, the core and central thrust of the Gospel for her times. I have elsewhere described this complex process, involving as it does the entire Christian community, the Scriptures and eventually the authorities in the Church.[18] The core of the Gospel, we conclude, does not remain immobile. The task of reinterpretation depends on the Church's discernment of what the core and central thrust of the Gospel is for her own age.

The reinterpretation of doctrine, preserving the self-identity of the Gospel, we conclude, is not a purely rational process, not a logical, psychological, or metaphysical construction. It is a vital process. It includes the Church's own religious experience. It takes place as Christians, seeking fidelity to the Christ they have encountered, understand themselves and their mission in a new way. At such times the Church will enter a crisis in regard to her truth. Only as Christians continue to listen to God's Word, take their own religious experience seriously, and engage in conversation with the whole community, will the Church gain a new self-understanding and acquire a secure perspective on the Gospel.[19]

In this process of reinterpretation, the Christian people rely on a special gift to the Church, operative within her and finding expression in authoritative pronouncements. Without this gift, the Gospel of Christ cannot be preserved and proclaimed. What are we to call this gift of truth?

Hans Küng, we recall, used the term "indefectibility". It seems to me, however, that he did not sufficiently appreciate the creative role the Spirit plays in the transmission of the Gospel from age to age. For Küng the guidance of the Spirit was operative in the Church's willingness to apply a biblical critique to her teaching and practice and thus bring forth principles of her own self-correction. This overlooks God's ongoing self-communication in the Church, enabling her to discern the focal point of the Gospel in new historical situations.

I see no reason why this special gift should not be called "infallibility".[20] It is true that Vatican I meant something much wider and more precise. Vatican I tried to give witness to God's presence in the Church's doctrine by making use of a slightly rationalistic model of truth. This model is no longer acceptable to us. But if we replace this model by the historical understanding of truth, referred to in these pages, the witness of Vatican I affirms a gift of truth, given to the Church including her authorities, which enables her to protect the self-identity of the Gospel by formulating it anew when the spirituo-cultural conditions of life demand it. While we separate ourselves from the literal meaning of Vatican I, we preserve and affirm its essential Christian witness. Thanks to this special gift of truth, the Church is able to take her own religious experience seriously, discern the center of the Gospel in her age, and reinterpret her dogma in its light as a message that continues to address people, that makes sense to them, and that initiates them into a new consciousness. Something of this took place at Vatican II! This gift of infallibility enables the Church to remain in God's truth and to utter it in power. But whether these utterances of truth take place in pronouncements that should be called infallible, I do not know. Vatican II certainly did not claim infallibility for its utterance of the Good News.

NOTES

1. *Infallible? An Inquiry*, New York, 1971. In the following we refer to this work as *Inf.*
2. *Inf.*, pp. 209-217.
3. The word "conversation" is used here in a wider sense than is customary. It is important to realize that every form of communication is addressed to someone and that its meaning depends on the historical situation of both the communicator and the receiver. It is, therefore, always part of a conversation.
4. *Inf.*, pp. 144-56.
4a. The English translation of Küng's book obscures this fact.

The German "Satz" is always rendered as "proposition" while its more general meaning is sentence or statement.

5. See especially *Dogma unter dem Wort Gottes*, Mainz, 1965.
6. Cf. *Inf.*, pp. 123, 160.
7. 95 (1970) 361-377.
8. 96 (1971) 43-64, 105-122.
9. 96 (1971) 145-160.
10. See my article "Bishop Simons and Development of Doctrine," *The Ecumenist*, 7 (Nov.-Dec., 1968) 6-12.
11. George Lindbeck, in his article in *America*, April 24, 1971, pp. 431-32, alludes to the influence of Hegel on Hans Küng's thought. Yet it seems to me that the Hegelian tradition is represented, rather, by Rahner and the theologians who uphold the ongoing self-revelation of God in history and hence defend the need for an ongoing reinterpretation of dogma, from one meaning to the next, yet preserving self-identity. Hans Küng remains aloof from this Hegelian trend when he restricts God's revelation to Israel and Jesus Christ, denies it for the Church's history, and consequently makes a radical distinction between "Word of God" and "human witness" and between "divine institution" and "historical development" (cf. *Inf.*, pp. 82, 217). A theologian in a Hegelian tradition does not exclude the possibility that a human testimony be Word of God and that an historical development be a divine institution. Küng does refer to Hegel in his new book, but only to remind the reader how problematic is the sharp separation of object and subject and how inadequate a static understanding of their interrelation (*Inf.*, p. 116, note 3). This aspect of Hegel's thought has been followed by many German philosophers and social scientists and is paralleled by thinkers in the English-speaking world, who regard reality as process. Again, this trend is much less pronounced in Küng than in the writings of Rahner and the theologians who regard divine revelation as constitutive, though gratuitously, of human history and the cosmos. It is true that for Küng the question whether the teaching of Vatican I was true "could presumably [according to Hegel] be answered only with Yes *and* No" (*Inf.*, p. 168). But he makes no attempt to assign a positive role to error and negation in the development of doctrine and thus to construct a Hegelian dialectic as has been done, in a tentative way, by Anselm Atkins in his "Doctrinal Development and Dialectic" *Continuum*, 6 (1968) 3-23. In reference to a possible Hegelian influence on Küng, see also note 16.
12. It was one of Yves Congar's special merits to have brought out, in his learned treatises, the practical and concrete nature of the Christian tradition. Thanks largely to him, Vatican II

was able to acknowledge tradition as "the Church, in her teaching, life and worship, perpetuating and handing on to all generations all that she is, all that she believes" (*On Divine Revelation*, n. 8).

13. April 9, 1971.

14. Some theologians regard such a definition of doctrine as anti-intellectual. Against it, they wish to defend the noetic aspect of Christian faith. Carl J. Peter, for instance, thinks that such a view of doctrine makes Christian faith simply an experience or an event in a person's life and hence neglects the truth-aspect traditionally associated with this faith (*Proceedings of the 25th Annual Convention of the Catholic Theological Society of America*, New York, 1971, pp. 188-89). In this perspective, however, faith is not simply an experience; it is, rather, a new consciousness, a special awareness of oneself as woven into a wider reality. To say that dogma is symbolic implies that it is meant to produce a special human self-understanding. This faith-consciousness includes a noetic component—just as self-knowledge does—but the knowledge it communicates is not that of an object. The neotic component of faith is that *it makes sense*, that it sheds light on human existence and the world, and makes the believer more aware of the presence of the divine mystery in human life and the cosmos.

15. For Rahner, divine revelation takes place in man on a pre-conceptual level and creates a new consciousness in him. The deepest self-communication of God to man, implicit in his life and grounding his quest for truth, is made more conscious, though never exhaustively so, through Christian doctrine. Dogma thematizes divine revelation present in unthematized fashion in the self-creation of man. Yet Rahner does not draw all the conclusions from this position that, in my opinion, follow from it.

16. Küng recognizes the historicity of truth. "Every proposition can be true *and* false—according as it is aimed, situated and intended" (*Inf.*, p. 172; the clarification of the translation is mine). George Lindbeck (*America*, April 24, 1971, p. 431) finds this a puzzling statement, reminiscent of Hegel's denial of the law of non-contradiction and possibly undermining the logic of all human discourse. Küng's sentence, however, is the simple acknowledgment that the meaning of a sentence cannot be determined apart from its context. This is a basic hermeneutical principle. The proposition "Jesus is man" can, in one context, affirm the Church's traditional teaching and, in another, be a denial of Jesus' divinity. It is Karl Rahner, rather than Hans Küng, however, who has reflected extensively on the historicity of truth.

17. In his study on the reformability of dogma (*Proceedings of the*

25th Annual Convention of the Catholic Theological Society of America, New York, 1971, pp. 111-136, and the abbreviated version, *The Survival of Dogma*, New York, 1971, pp. 185-203), Avery Dulles examines the positions of Rahner, Schillebeeckx, and Dewart and shows that the theological trend, so widely spread today, goes back to a reflection on historicity, suppressed during the Modernist crisis and formulated again, in a more nuanced way, by the theologians of *la nouvelle théologie*. He quotes from Henri Bouillard: "Christian truth never subsists in a pure state. By this we do not mean that it must inevitably be presented mingled with error, but that it is always embedded in contingent notions and schemes which determine its rational structure. It cannot be isolated from these. It can be liberated from one system of truth only by passing into another. . . ." (*The Survival of Dogma*, p. 187).

18. Cf. *The Credibility of the Church Today*, New York, 1968, chapter 4.

19. Doctrinal development, therefore, is not simply the passage from the implicit to the explicit. Quantum leaps do occur. In various terminologies this is being said by a growing number of theologians. Recently Avery Dulles has suggested that the very "form" of faith changes in different ages and that the Catholic Church has just left behind one form and found a new one, in which God's Word is present to it (*The Survival of Dogma*, pp. 17-31). It is a significant decision of the theologian studying critical issues such as infallibility *whether* he wants to solve them by extending the inherited notions one step further and hence remain in conceptual continuity with the past or *whether* he holds that something new has taken place, that the traditional notions will not do to render an account of the critical issues, and hence is willing to find new terms, discontinuous with the old, to deal with the issues raised. This decision is crucial. It pervades the theologian's entire work, influences his conclusions, and makes itself known to the reader unmistakably like a perfume. The basic decision where one stands historically, whether in times of continuity or in revolutionary, discontinuous times, affects all the human sciences, including history and sociology (cf. E. Troeltsch, *Der Historismus und seine Probleme*, Tübingen, 1922, p. 112).

20. At the centennial celebration of Vatican I held in Rome in January, 1970, Paul de Vooght, known as a moderate theologian, stated: "Infallibility does not consist in a power to express irreformable formulas, but in a power to reformulate throughout the centuries a number (a very limited number at that) of essential Christian truths." Quoted by Michael Fahey, *America*, April 24, 1971, p. 430. See also my *Faith and Doctrine*, New York, 1969, p. 132.

Richard
McBRIEN

I have divided this essay into two unequal parts: the one critical, the other systematic.

In the first, and shorter, section I address myself directly to some specific items in the book under review, indicating where I am in agreement and where I am not. Most of my comments in this first part do not go deeply into the issues. In large measure they serve only to catalogue what I regard to be the plusses and minuses of Hans Küng's book. I leave to one or another of my fellow contributors the task of closer textual analysis, exegesis, and criticism.

The second part of this essay attempts a fuller systematic, although still largely tentative, discussion of papal infallibility. The presentation poses neither as a corrective nor even as an alternative to Küng's position. It will be clear that I am already fundamentally sympathetic with his views. However, it seems important that the issue of infallibility should be studied from a perspective larger than the phenomenon of *Humanae Vitae* or even of the crisis of ecclesiastical leadership. The most appropriate ecclesiological context, it seems to me, is that of the nature and mission of the Church itself, within which context problems such as the papal encyclical and papal, curial, episcopal, and pastoral intransigence emerge as essentially subordinate questions.

I shall be proposing eight theses, some of which will overlap with Küng's presentation and some of which, particularly the seventh, Küng did not seem to raise at all. It may be useful to have these eight theses on the record before the review of *Infallible? An Inquiry,* since my comments on the book itself may make more sense if my theological presuppositions are already in clear view.

1. The traditional definition of papal infallibility is frequently misunderstood, and this is the fault especially of theologians themselves who have tended to exaggerate its meaning and therefore to distort the original intention of Vatican I.

2. There is no adequate biblical or historical basis for the dogma of papal infallibility. This does not necessarily mean that the dogma is wrong, but there *is* an abiding responsibility on the part of Catholic theologians to defend this dogma and it is becoming increasingly difficult to do so on the basis of biblical and historical materials.

3. The ecumenicity of the dogma of papal infallibility is proportionate to the ecumenicity of the council which promulgated it. If we are to accept the ecclesiology of Vatican II that the Body of Christ embraces, in varying degrees, the whole Christian community and not the Catholic Church alone, then it follows that the Body of Christ was not adequately represented at the nineteenth century council and that such a council can be called "ecumenical" in a limited, perhaps even analogical, sense.

4. It does not seem that the mission of the Church requires papal infallibility in the sense proposed by Vatican I. The extraordinarily sparse exercise of this charism is indicative of its relative unimportance and even uselessness.

5. The traditional notion of papal infallibility does not adequately take into account the multiple meaning of revelation: as word, as event, as existential encounter, and as promise.

6. The validity of the doctrine of papal infallibility must stand or fall on its own merits. It cannot simply be identified with indefectibility since these two realities, although closely related, are not one and the same.

7. (a) There is a hierarchy of truths attested to by the Decree on Ecumenism, n. 11. Papal infallibility does not seem

to merit occupancy at, or near, the top of the list. It is certainly not necessary for living participation in the Body of Christ, otherwise we should have to revert to the ecclesiological assumptions of Pope Pius XII in *Humani Generis*.

(b) Neither does it seem to be necessary for communion with the Catholic Church, since such communion is based on the larger issue of the understanding and exercise of collegiality. Collegiality includes the papal office, to be sure, but one can legitimately affirm the Petrine office without necessarily affirming the charism of papal infallibility, even when that charism is restricted by the various conditions imposed by Vatican I. The Church throughout most of its life was precisely in that situation, i.e., it functioned as the Body of Christ without reference to the infallibility of the pope.

8. Hans Küng is essentially right in his criticism of the traditional notion of papal infallibility and in reaffirming indefectibility as the basis of Christian fidelity to Christ and to his Gospel (or, more accurately, as the basis of God's fidelity to the Church). This position, as Küng himself suggests, has significant ecumenical possibilities.

I. Infallible? An Inquiry: Some Critical Reflections

I should agree with Hans Küng that the renewal of the Catholic Church has been thwarted frequently by ecclesiastical officials who have apparently never accepted nor understood the significance of the Second Vatican Council and the spirit which the council not only unleashed but also symbolized (pp. 12-30); [1] that the Petrine office can provide an important and, indeed, an irreplaceable service to the Church, as John XXIII demonstrated so effectively (pp. 27 and 109); that the principal concern behind *Humanae Vitae* was ideological rather than theological, i.e., that the pope and the commission's minority regarded the credibility of the magisterium as the principal value at stake (p. 62); that episcopal infallibility was inadequately established by the Second Vatican Council (pp. 79 ff.); that apostolic succession applies, in the first instance, to the whole Church (p. 82); that bishops are not the "sole teachers" in a diocese or in the Church at large, and that the office of bishop and the office of teacher can legitimately be separated (p. 84); that there were several non-theological motives behind the promulgation of the dogma of papal infallibility by the First Vatican Council (pp. 87 ff.); that the biblical arguments for papal infallibility as well as the arguments from tradition are simply not persuasive (pp. 109-121); that the various doctrinal formulations regarding the papacy and Mariology were unnecessarily provocative in an ecumenical sense (p. 149); that the binding character of a formulation of faith does not depend upon its immunity from error (p. 151); that the spirit of rationalism had much to do with the emergence of an infallibility-mentality in the nineteenth century (pp. 162-169); that the notion of indefectibility is more adequately grounded in Scripture and tradition than is the notion of papal infallibility (pp. 175 and 181); that the notion of infallibility-as-indefectibility has significant ecumenical possibilities vis-à-vis Lutherans (pp. 195-196), Calvinists (p. 197), and Anglicans (pp. 197-198); that the critique of papal infallibility must extend to the definitions of ecumenical councils (pp. 200-208) and even to the formulations of Sacred Scripture (pp. 209-211); that the ground of our Christian faith is not the Bible or even the Church but the God who reveals himself in Jesus Christ as attested to by Sacred Scripture and as encountered in the human community, in general, and the Christian community, in particular (pp. 218-219); that bishops and other pastoral officers exercise a ministry of leadership in the Church but such leadership does not require all of the traditional (post-Vatican I) notions of papal and episcopal magisterium (pp. 222-240).

Certain of these areas of agreement are, of course, more important than others. I shall expand some of these points in the second, systematic part.

In the spirit of St. Augustine, Küng asks his critics to correct him if they judge that he is mistaken. There are several items which require some comment and I am limiting myself here to five of them.

1. I agree with Avery Dulles and others that Küng is mistaken when he argues that the teaching of *Humanae Vitae* and the doctrine of papal infallibility stand or fall together.[2] Küng insists that the encyclical fulfills the requirements for an infallible pronouncement and, since the encyclical is in error, we are faced with a dilemma: either we must accept the papal condemnation of contraception or we must reject the dogma of papal infallibility (pp. 67-68). *Humanae Vitae* is, in his judgment, the "Achilles heel" of the Roman doctrine of infallibility (p. 176).

Küng certainly knows that this encyclical does not fulfill all of the conditions for an infallible pronouncement as set down by Vatican I. Indeed, in his earlier work, *Structures of the Church*, he wrote: "(The pope) is infallible *only* when, as the universal teacher and supreme judge of the Church, he purposes to define, in the strictest sense and with the claim of his whole authority, a final doctrinal decision in matters of faith and morals for the whole Church. Gasser emphatically features the word 'only' (*solummodo*). Thus *all* conditions without exception must be fulfilled and surely and solidly established before one can talk of an infallible definition. Hence the CIC [Code of Canon Law] also definitely states: 'Unless expressly stated no matter is held as declared or dogmatically defined' (c. 1323, n. 3)." [3]

By insisting that *Humanae Vitae* must be treated as an infallible pronouncement, Küng forces us to raise the question: which notion of papal infallibility is he criticizing in this book—the notion carefully defined by Vatican I or the notion generally accepted by ultramontane theologians and various ecclesiastical officials?

The case against papal infallibility as defined by the First Vatican Council does not depend upon our acceptance of Küng's view that *Humanae Vitae* is an infallible teaching. Nevertheless, Küng seems unnecessarily to confuse, and thereby weaken, the argument by posing the issue in terms of a basically false dilemma: either accept *Humanae Vitae* or reject papal infallibility.

2. The second point of disagreement is closely related to

the first. I should suggest that Küng's assertion that Vatican I accorded to the pope power without limit ("But the teaching of Vatican I really amounts to this: if he wants, the pope can do everything, even without the Church.") is completely unwarranted (p. 105). I do not question for a moment that such is the thinking of many Catholics, inside and outside of the hierarchy, but the object of criticism here must be the official teaching of the Church and not the conventional wisdom of many contemporary Catholics.

In *Structures of the Church* Küng specifically raises the problem: what happens if the pope sets himself arbitrarily against the Church? Could he define a dogma *"contra consensum ecclesiae?"* "Under no circumstances," he responds forthrightly. "Despite all emphasis on papal full authority Vatican I repeatedly attached a great importance to the fact that no conflict situations could arise between the pope and the Church (episcopate). Even the pope who formulates a definition is morally obliged—harkening to the voice of the Church—to guard himself from a schism that might arise, 'if he does not want to have union with the whole body of the Church and be connected with her as he should'." [4]

And in his more recent work, *The Church,* he reaffirms this position: "Since the definition of the primacy has often been misunderstood the elucidations of it emerging from the Council documents are of importance. They show that papal primacy, even in the view of Vatican I, is by no means an arbitrary absolutism, but rather that:

"1. The power of the pope is not absolute *(absolute monarchica).*
"2. The power of the pope is not arbitrary *(arbitraria).*
"3. The power of the pope has its limits *(limitatio);* it is limited actively by Christ, passively by the apostles and their successors. The pope is also limited as a matter of course by the natural law *(ius naturale)* and divine law *(ius divina).*
"4. The concrete limits of the exercise of primacy are: (a) the existence of the episcopate, which the pope

can neither abolish nor dissolve as regards its position or its rights; (b) the ordinary exercise of office by the bishops; in no case may the pope, being as it were another bishop, intervene in the daily exercise of office by the bishops; (c) the aim of the pope's exercise of office; its constant aim must be the edification and the unity of the Church; (d) the manner of papal exercise of office; it must not be arbitrary, inopportune or exaggerated, but must be dictated by the needs and the evident benefit of the Church." [5]

Later in the same section Küng alludes to the principle of subsidiarity as set forth by Pope Pius XI in *Quadragesimo Anno* and as endorsed by Pope Pius XII and the Declaration on Religious Freedom (n. 7) of the Second Vatican Council. Applied to the question of papal authority and the exercise thereof, the principle of subsidiarity means: "as much freedom as possible, curtailed only as much as is necessary." [6]

I should agree again with Father Dulles' remark that "this interpretation of infallibility [namely, that Vatican I gave the pope a kind of blank check] gives Küng a wide target to shoot at, but in the end it weakens his case, for moderate infallibilists will say that Küng has not hit the only target they would be interested in defending." [7]

3. Just as the majority on the papal commission did not deal directly enough with the question that bothered the pope (namely, the continuity of papal teachings and the credibility of the papal magisterium), so Küng does not deal directly enough with the question that bothers his critics, including Rahner: What is the basis of Catholic identity if it is not belief in the infallibility of the pope? [8]

Positively, Küng should have indicated that communion with the Catholic Church has to do primarily with our understanding and exercise of collegiality and only secondarily with the canonical structuring of the collegial principle. Negatively, he should have indicated that rejection of papal infallibility, as traditionally defined and understood, does not necessarily undermine this communion with the Catholic Church nor does it contradict one's commitment to the Catholic tradition. I shall return to this issue later, in the discussion of my seventh thesis.

There is indeed a certain ambiguity, edging perhaps towards ambivalence, in Küng's Catholic self-understanding. I have in mind especially his recent *America* article, "Why I Am Staying in the Church." [9] He provides two reasons: the first and fundamental reason is theological; the second and apparently subordinate reason is personal.

He states his "decisive answer" in the following way: "I am staying in the Church because I have been convinced by Jesus Christ and all that He stands for, and because the Church-community, despite all of its failures, pleads the cause of Jesus Christ and must continue to do so." The article concludes with this sentence: "I am staying in the Church *because* I am a Christian."

And the second reason: "I have received too much from this community of faith to be able to leave so easily. I have been too involved in Church reform and renewal to be willing to disappoint those who have been involved with me."

"To those opposed to renewal," he continues, "I do not want to give the pleasure of my leaving; to the partisans of renewal, I do not want to give the pain."

The problem is which question does Küng answer in his article: (1) Why should one remain a Christian? or (2) Why should one remain a Catholic?

He assumes throughout the essay that by answering the first question he is also answering the second. But that is simply not the case unless, of course, we are to assert that within the Body of Christ there is nothing distinctive about the Catholic experience and tradition.

The *America* article is truly a moving account of one theologian's decision to reaffirm his affiliation with the Body of Christ because it is the Body of Christ alone which, in season and out of season, confesses the Lordship of Jesus and commits itself explicitly to the realization of his Gospel among men. But the article does not yet confront the questions: Why remain in the *Catholic* Church? Why not move to some other portion of the Body of Christ where one no longer has to explain away the policies and attitudes of the pope, the curia, and hundreds of bishops?

The only point at which Küng struggles with the specifically Catholic question, and then indirectly, is with his acknowledgement of responsibility to other Catholics who have been involved with him in the renewal movement. Being a Catholic, it seems, means having fashioned and fostered personal relationships with a particular group of people. To be other than Catholic is to have other than Catholic associations. To leave the Catholic Church is to leave the fellowship of Catholic people.

I do not wish to imply that Küng says this, but I do insist that he says no more than that when it comes to the unspoken question, "Why stay in the *Catholic* Church?"

4. I do not know why Hans Küng did not challenge the ecumenicity of Vatican I. I think that he should have done so. Indeed, he has argued that "the *ecumenicity* of a council is *not a priori certain*" (p. 203). This might have been usefully developed, but it was not. I shall offer some comment on the possibility of questioning the ecumenicity of Vatican I in the discussion of my third thesis.

5. Küng fails to acknowledge the change in his own position from *Structures of the Church* and *The Church,* on the one hand, to *Infallible? An Inquiry,* on the other. He gives the impression that he regards his latest book as an exceedingly logical, consistent development of his earlier works. Undoubtedly much of the material in *Infallible?* has its academic grounding in these earlier, more scholarly volumes, but on the central issue Küng has changed his mind. Where once he affirmed papal infallibility, under the conditions specified by Vatican I, he now rejects it. The position that he once characterized as "Protestant" he now adopts as his own.

"For Protestant Christians," he wrote, "the continuity and indestructibility of the Church does not depend upon the infallibility of certain utterances but upon the Spirit, which operatively permeates the frailty and fallibility of human beings as well as their utterances. . . ." [10] This is the position which Küng himself now defends.

I do not suggest that the credibility of Hans Küng's theological credentials is finally undermined by his change of view on papal infallibility, any more than the credibility of the papal magisterium would have been finally undermined by a change of view on the morality of contraception. Nevertheless, Küng might usefully have confronted this change in his own thinking more directly than he appears to do.

II. Papal Infallibility: Ecclesiological Reflections

·Thesis #1: *The traditional definition of papal infallibility is frequently misunderstood, and this is the fault especially of theologians themselves who have tended to exaggerate its meaning and therefore to distort the original intention of Vatican I.*

In a recent exchange with Cardinal Joseph Höffner of Cologne, Karl Rahner wrote, "I ask where the bishops have learned their theology if not from the theologians. . . ." [11] A sample of the kind of theology many bishops and other Catholics have received—and continue to accept uncritically—is available in J. Salaverri's *Sacrae Theologicae Summa,* a textbook series that has enjoyed wide international circulation in Catholic seminaries for many years.

Salaverri's views are pertinent here because they are taken at face value in Küng's book. It is on the basis of such theology that Küng ascribed infallibility to *Humanae Vitae.* Judgment of the "orthodoxy" of Catholic theologians on the question of papal primacy and papal infallibility is often measured by the theologian's proximity to, or distance from, the position marked out by the so-called *Spanish Summa.*

Salaverri, it seems to me, is guilty of serious exaggeration on two major points: (1) He extends infallibility to the ordinary magisterium of the pope (i.e., he argues that the pope can be infallible even when his pronouncement does not fulfill the conditions established by Vatican I as, for example, when he issues an encyclical letter, taking a stand on an important dogmatic or moral issue, but never explicitly appealing to the charism of infallibility nor explicitly declaring that he intends to bind the whole Church to this teaching);[12] and (2) he extends infallibility to the so-called secondary objects, such as liturgical decrees, the canonization of saints, the approval of rules and constitutions of religious orders, and so forth.[13]

Catholic theologians as temperamentally moderate and as academically cautious as Gustave Thils and Yves Congar have characterized these views, especially the former (relating to the ordinary magisterium), as excessive and certainly not required by the teaching of Vatican I. Thils acknowledges, in fact, that such views have unnecessarily exacerbated ecumenical dialogue on the papal question and, more radically, do not seem to be in keeping with the careful wording of the conciliar text and of the official interpretation of that text by Bishop Gasser. The pope is infallible only when (*solummodo . . . quando*) he is defining according to the conditions specified by Vatican I.[14] Salaverri's position, so widely circulated by various bishops in the aftermath of *Humanae Vitae* when they argued that Catholics must respond to this encyclical "as if" it were an infallible pronouncement because "for all practical purposes" it is infallible, has not enjoyed the same widespread support among his fellow ecclesiologists. On the contrary, the thesis that infallibility extends to the ordinary magisterium of the pope is generally rejected by Catholic theologians today.[15]

Congar's position is similar to Thils'. He, too, notes with approval the general rejection of Salaverri's thesis. He reminds us that Vatican I never treated the question of the ordinary magisterium of the pope and that the post-Vatican I developments in this regard—reaching their high-point during the pontificate of Pius XII—are pathological: the theological abuse of infallibility has the same pathological relationship to truth as legalism has to morality.[16]

Catholics should have already made a considerable advance, theologically and ecumenically, if they are at least prepared to reject the Salaverri view. Unfortunately Hans Küng's book and his use of Salaverri's argument with regard to *Humanae Vitae* may give that argument a longer life span than it deserves, because some Catholics may be led to construct a false dilemma of their own: either accept Salaverri's view and remain faithful to the Church or accept Küng's and place yourself outside the Church.

Thesis #2: *There is no adequate biblical or historical basis for the dogma of papal infallibility. This does not necessarily mean that the dogma is wrong, but there is an abiding responsibility on the part of Catholic theologians to defend this dogma and it is becoming increasingly difficult to do so on the basis of biblical and historical materials.*

Salaverri proves first the infallibility of the episcopate and then the infallibility of the pope. Significantly, he makes no case at all for the infallibility of the whole Church.

The- proof for the infallibility of the episcopate, whether in the exercise of their extraordinary or ordinary magisteria, is drawn from previous doctrinal formulations. There is an occasional indirect reference to the New Testament, but none of these are brought forth as a proof for infallibility as such. The pertinent source is Denzinger, not Sacred Scripture.[17]

He proves papal infallibility from episcopal infallibility, with additional references to Mt 16:18f. and Jn 21:15-17. The Roman Pontiff is by the will of Christ the supreme pastor of the Church. This means that he possesses whatever power resides in the Church. But the highest kind of doctrinal power which is in the Church is infallibility. Therefore, the Roman Pontiff, as the rock, the bearer of the keys of the Kingdom, and as universal pastor has infallibility.[18]

He makes a specific case on the basis of Mt 16:18-19 where his major assumption in each of two syllogisms is that the Church is an essentially doctrinal society (*societate essentialiter doctrinali*). The Gospel texts establish the primacy of the Roman Pontiff. But his primacy cannot be effective for the unity and strength of the Church if he cannot teach infallibly. Therefore the pope is infallible. A similar kind of argument is drawn from Lk 22:32.[19]

Salaverri's argument, it seems to me, fails on two counts: it approaches the New Testament almost fundamentalistically and, secondly, it makes assumptions about the nature and mission of the Church which are difficult to sustain, especially in the light of the ecclesiological developments of the last decade.[20]

Further indication of the weakness of the traditional biblical arguments for papal infallibility is provided in the article on infallibility by H. Fries and J. Finsterhölzl in *Sacramentum Mundi*.[21] The section, "Biblical Foundations," is remarkable for its brevity and tentative character. The authors describe "the starting-point" of papal infallibility as the promise of the Lord, who is himself the truth (Jn 1:14; 14:6; 1 Jn 5:20) and who entrusted to his community the word of truth. They regard as "the most important proofs" the farewell discourses in John's Gospel, especially the promise of the Paraclete as the Spirit of truth (Jn 14:17; 15:26; 16:13). They refer also to 1 Tim 3:15 where the text supposedly speaks of the Church as "pillar and the ground of truth." I say "supposedly" because the recent Congar article on infallibility and indefectibility, to which I have already referred, reminds us that the meaning of this text is controverted. Congar cites a recent study by A. Jaubert which argues that the text applies to Timothy himself and not to the Church.[22]

Fries and Finsterhölzl conclude: "to sum up, it may be said that the post-Easter community reflected on the reliability of its faith and preaching, and took cognizance of the promise and of its duty to remain in the truth." [23] I should argue, however, that the biblical data supports, at most, the indefectibility of the Church, namely that the Spirit of the Lord will so abide with the Church throughout its life that, over the long run of history, it will not fall from fidelity to Christ or to his Gospel. To have established the indefectibility of the Church (if such texts do, in fact, establish it) is not necessarily to have established the infallibility of the Church, of the bishops, or of the pope, in such wise that each of these three subjects is preserved from all possible error in every single instance of a solemn, official, doctrinal promulgation. The notion of indefectibility does not require this, and the biblical texts do not seem to prove more than indefectibility.

The case from history is no more persuasive. I should refer the reader to Yves Congar's *L'Eglise de saint Augustin à l'époque moderne* which, unintentionally or not, demonstrates the weakness of the argument from tradition for papal infallibility. Even in the period of the most intense papal fervor, the Middle Ages, there is no evidence of an explicit teaching on papal infallibility. What is always at issue is the indefectibility of the Church rather than the infallibility of any agency within the Church. Indeed, the Roman Church itself not only can err, in the judgment of the Church of the Middle Ages, but the Roman Church has erred as a matter of fact. It was generally recognized that the pope could fall into heresy and that, when he does, he ceases *ipso facto* to be head of the Church. Congar concludes, on the basis of his study of the theological and doctrinal materials of the Middle Ages, that the dogma of 1870 cannot be found in this period except germinally.

Even at the beginning of the sixteenth century, there is abundant evidence of uncertainty regarding the primacy of the pope by divine right and particularly regarding his infallibility. (Papal infallibility, after all, was not even an issue during the Protestant Reformation!) The question remained unsettled and disputed until the middle of the nineteenth century when, of course, a definitive decision was taken by the First Vatican Council.[24]

Küng himself makes a strong case against the traditional historical arguments, particularly by linking St. Thomas Aquinas' defense of papal infallibility with his uncritical reliance upon the False Decretals.

While it is true that the method of Catholic dogmatic theology requires that the Catholic theologian accept a dogmatic formulation as "given" (rather than challenge it as if the formulation were never made by an ecumenical council of the Church), it is also true that the theologian's first duty is to the truth and, only secondarily, to the Church. The dogma of papal infallibility has come into question in a new way in recent years. Charles Davis' challenge to Catholic orthodoxy on this and other topics was set forth just after the Second Vatican Council. Bishop Simons issued his own position paper in

1968, and now we have Hans Küng's work. The dogma may certainly be "in possession" for the Catholic theologian, but that does not mean in any sense that the dogma is beyond the range of criticism or even beyond the very possibility of radical revision and/or rejection.

It must somehow be explained why a dogma with such weak biblical and historical support should remain, for many Catholics, a kind of touchstone of Catholic orthodoxy. Do we continue to affirm the dogma only because of the consequences of its rejection, or do we continue to affirm the dogma because we are convinced that it is true and that it is of great value to the Church, for the sake of her mission? It seems that we are faced with the same kind of dilemma that confronted the pope and his advisers prior to *Humanae Vitae*. If the choice is difficult for Catholic theologians today, that should at least give them a sense of sympathy for the pope's own dilemma a few years ago.

Thesis #3: *The ecumenicity of the dogma of papal infallibility is proportionate to the ecumenicity of the council which promulgated it. If we are to accept the ecclesiology of Vatican II that the Body of Christ embraces, in varying degrees, the whole Christian community and not the Catholic Church alone, then it follows that the Body of Christ was not adequately represented at the nineteenth century council and that such a council can be called "ecumenical" in a limited, perhaps even analogical, sense.*

Theologically, an ecumenical council is a gathering of the whole Church in order to face a problem confronting the whole Church and to propose a solution, doctrinal or disciplinary, that might apply, as far as possible, to the whole Church. Hypothetically, every member of the Church should attend an ecumenical council, since the Church itself is an ecumenical council called together by God in his Spirit.[25] Realistically, such councils must be representative. Each member of the Church is present at the council through his or her pastor. Again hypothetically, every Christian holding pastoral office in the Church should attend an ecumenical council in order to insure the widest possible representation, for every pastor is, in a real theological sense, a bishop. The only difference between a pastor and a bishop is in the extent of responsibility. A pastor is the overseer of a given Eucharistic community; a bishop is the overseer of a cluster of Eucharistic communities. Again realistically, the representatives of the Church at an ecumenical council must be limited somehow if the assembly is to be manageable and effective. Thus, the Church has traditionally restricted direct and deliberative participation in ecumenical councils to bishops.

However, there is another crucial theological principle which is relevant here and which is usually not discussed at all. An ecumenical council, aside from the particular system of representation, must reflect and embrace the whole Church. All Christians must participate, at least through representatives, if a council is to be regarded as truly ecumenical. Since the Church is not restricted to the Roman Catholic Church alone, a council is truly and fully ecumenical when the representatives of all Christian churches are present and active in its deliberations.[26]

Indeed, Küng says this in his *Structures of the Church* but he fails here, as he fails in *Infallible? An Inquiry,* to draw the necessary conclusion about Vatican I: "The *Catholic* Church would not be credibly represented if at ecumenical councils by human convocation all the individual Churches, with their specific histories and their traditions, with their problems and needs, their objections and concerns, their wishes and demands, were denied full expression. . . . The Catholic Church is credibly represented when, on the one hand, all individual Churches can integrate their particularity with the decisions of a council as a whole." [27]

The ecumenicity of Vatican I is not *a priori* certain. On the contrary, the limitation of representation to the Catholic communion raises positive doubts about the council's ecumenicity and, therefore, about the ecumenicity of its dogmatic formulations. The hundred year period following the council seems to confirm this judgment. The papal definitions have never been accepted by any of the other Christian churches and now we are finding some signs of uneasiness and uncertainty even within the Catholic Church.

If the case for papal infallibility is already difficult because of the sparseness of biblical and historical testimony, then it is made even more difficult if the only surviving argument, i.e., from the authority of the First Vatican Council, is subject to radical challenge. I should suggest that it *is* subject to challenge.[28]

Thesis #4: *It does not seem that the mission of the Church requires papal infallibility in the sense proposed by Vatican I. The extraordinary sparse exercise of this charism is indicative of its relative unimportance and even uselessness.*

Sometimes one gets the impression that papal infallibility functions in the same way as the stockpiling of nuclear weapons as a deterrent to their eventual use by the other side. Political leaders will insist that they have no intention of ever using these weapons. Then why have them at all? Because without them one country would be at the mercy of the others that do have them. The same kind of reasoning seems to be applied to papal infallibility. Of course the pope is not infallible in a permanent or personal way but only when he is in the act of defining a dogma of faith under the conditions carefully listed by Vatican I. For all practical purposes the charism will never be invoked except possibly for experimental purposes (was the dogma of the Assumption the "Nevada testing" of the charism?).

The Pastoral Constitution on the Church in the Modern World characterized the arms race, with its explicit motives of deterrence, as "an utterly treacherous trap for humanity. . . . It is much to be feared that if this race persists, it will eventually spawn all the lethal ruin whose path it is now making ready." [29]

The extension of the definition of papal infallibility to various secondary objects (canonization of saints, etc.) and especially to the exercise of the ordinary magisterium (papal encyclicals, etc.) shows how treacherous indeed is this infallibility-mentality. A charism which is never used (or used only in a largely irrelevant area as in the dogma of the Assumption) cannot possibly be regarded as essential in any way to the mission of the Church, despite the arguments of Salaverri and others in the past.

I agree with Charles Davis when he says that "an infallible intervention by the pope is conceivable only when there is no longer any need for its authority, because the problem belongs to the past and the results of the debate are secure. . . . That is why what may be called a practical infallibility has to be assigned to ordinary papal teaching in order to make papal authority actually operative." [30]

Some may want to argue, in rebuttal, that the actual exercise of infallibility has not been limited to the promulgation of the dogma of the Assumption, that many of the doctrinal formulations of earlier ecumenical councils fall within the conditions for an infallible pronouncement. I do not agree. Vatican I was explicit. It did not set down conditions for the exercise of the Church's infallibility or of an ecumenical council's, but only of the pope's. Nowhere except in the case of the dogma of the Assumption are these conditions ostensibly fulfilled. Indeed, the dogma of the Assumption makes the dogmatic statement of Vatican I all the more problematic.

Furthermore, any kind of infallibility (papal, episcopal, or ecclesial in the broadest sense) is ultimately important only where consistent and persistent doctrinal uniformity and cognitive clarity are regarded as values of the highest order. This is the case with those whose view of the Church remains pre-Copernican (the Church, rather than the Kingdom of God, is at the center of history). The Church exists for salvation. Men are saved if they believe the truth. The truth, in turn, is proclaimed and authentically interpreted by the pope and bishops. Therefore, if one does not wish to jeopardize his salvation, he must adhere without qualification to whatever the pope and bishops teach. Distinctions between infallible and noninfallible statements are meaningless. The benefit of the doubt is to be accorded to the magisterial pronouncement. After all, it might be right, even though noninfallible, in which case it becomes another in a long line of truths necessary for salvation. To the pre-

Copernican mind every tiny portion of the total corpus of Christian doctrine is equally vital. For if, indeed, angels do not exist, and if the Church has taught at one time that angels *do* exist, then the whole network loses its credibility and we are no longer sure about what God wants us to believe in order to be saved.

This view exaggerates the importance of intellectual clarity and the assurance of the truth of doctrinal propositions. Catholic theologians such as Schillebeeckx, Dulles, and others are suggesting now that orthopraxy (right practice) is as important as orthodoxy (right belief), that without the former the latter is simply ideological.[31] Indefectibility has to do with both orthopraxy, i.e., with the long-term fidelity of the whole institutional Church to the demands of the Gospel, and orthodoxy, i.e., with the long-term fidelity of the whole institutional Church to the truth of the Gospel, despite occasional errors in individual instances.

Thesis #5: *The traditional notion of papal infallibility does not adequately take into account the multiple meaning of revelation: as word, as event, as existential encounter, and as promise.*

Catholic theologians, such as Gustave Thils and others, go to great lengths to insist against the Protestants, especially Karl Barth, that infallibility has nothing at all to do with the formulation of new revelation but only with the interpretation of what has already been handed down by God through his Church. This theme recurs continually throughout Thils' measured historical study of the Vatican dogma and is also emphasized by Küng himself in *Structures of the Church*.[32]

The problem is that revelation is not necessarily closed. It is not confined entirely to the past. The traditional notion of papal infallibility assumes that the charism is necessary for those rare moments (so rare, in fact, that they practically do not exist at all) when there is a dispute about the meaning of some aspect or another of the so-called deposit of faith. When the pope examines this essentially static, finished reality, he is guaranteed immunity from error in telling the rest of the Church what he sees in the treasure chest.

However, the theology of revelation in recent years has expanded considerably our previous understanding of the meaning and scope of God's self-disclosure in history. Revelation may be regarded as an ongoing, here-and-now reality, or even as something which is not yet fulfilled, in the manner of promise. The writings of Bultmann, Moran, Moltmann, and others embody these additional options.[33] If infallibility is for the sake of interpreting only what God has already said to man, then what charism is it that gives the same assurance of immunity from error in the revelation that is or that has not yet been?

Certainly the objection here is not insurmountable. One could say that revelation in any sense and in any tense (past, present, or future) can only be interpreted propositionally. The charism still applies. However, such an understanding of revelation was not in force at Vatican I and I have not yet seen any defender of the dogma of papal infallibility integrate that dogma with this newer, broader understanding of revelation. Küng makes some attempt at discussing the language problem, but his treatment is not completely successful.[34]

I am suggesting here that the dogma of papal infallibility is inextricably bound up with a limited notion of revelation (as well as a limited notion of the mission of the Church, if we are to take Salaverri's views as an example of the dogma's ecclesiological assumptions), and that this connection must enter into our judgment regarding the truth or falsity of the dogma, or at least regarding its appropriateness and value for the Church.

Thesis #6: *The validity of the doctrine of papal infallibility must stand or fall on its own merits. It cannot simply be identified with indefectibility since these two realities, although closely related, are not one and the same.*

There is a tendency sometimes to slide over the difference between infallibility and indefectibility, even by those who are prepared to define these two items as separate realities. I have Congar in mind. In referring to the theological sources of the Middle Ages Congar concludes that they (i.e., the medieval authors) "held essentially to the infallibility, *or better* (*ou plutôt*) to the indefectibility of the Church." [35] Congar explicitly discusses the relationship between infallibility and indefectibility in an article of the same title, but nowhere in the article does he make a real case for the former, only the latter. Even in the appended review of Küng's book (which appeared after Congar wrote the main body of the article), Congar criticizes not the heart of Küng's argument against papal infallibility but rather Küng's tendency to separate the ordained leadership of the Church from the rest of the community.[36]

I should suggest that even indefectibility is problematical, but it has more to support it in Sacred Scripture and history than infallibility. If Catholic theologians are now prepared to identify infallibility with indefectibility (as they often have done anyway in practice, and especially in popular presentations), then they should clearly understand what they are doing. It is not simply a matter of jettisoning the word "infallibility" which most are willing to do. The Vatican I definition of papal infallibility is not a definition of indefectibility as it applies to the pope. Indefectibility is for the long run and can tolerate individual errors and infidelities in preaching, in sacramental celebration, in community life, and in service to mankind. Infallibility is for the immediate, individual occasion when a particular doctrinal issue is at stake. Infallibility can tolerate no error of any kind, under any circumstances.

To question infallibility, however, is not to question indefectibility. Some may ask how the Church can be indefectible if, at some moment in its history, it can teach, with solemn authority, an erroneous interpretation of God's word. Can an indefectible Church lead the faithful into serious doctrinal error? I should suggest that the fidelity of the Church to the Gospel and to its mission can never be dependent on a single doctrinal pronouncement, no matter how solemnly it has been proposed. The authority and accuracy of a given pronouncement can only be measured by the long range effect it has upon the Church at large, over the long run of history. If the Church can be wrong about its faith in Jesus as Lord, one can certainly speak of its defectibility. If the Church—in this instance the Catholic Church—can be wrong about its judgment regarding papal infallibility, one cannot say that such an error would contradict the consistent testimony of the Body of Christ from its origins. The teaching on papal infallibility had few biblical or historical antecedents and evoked no favorable ecumenical response at all. If we must conclude today that Vatican I was in error in its dogma of papal infallibility, such a judgment need not compromise in any way the indefectibility of the Church.

Thesis #7: *(a) There is a hierarchy of truths attested to by the Decree on Ecumenism, n. 11. Papal infallibility does not seem to merit occupancy at, or near, the top of the list. It is certainly not necessary for living participation in the Body of Christ, otherwise we should have to revert to the ecclesiological assumptions of Pope Pius XII in* Humani Generis. *(b) Neither does it seem to be necessary for communion with the Catholic Church, since such communion is based on the larger issue of the understanding and exercise of collegiality. Collegiality includes the papal office, to be sure, but one can legitimately affirm the Petrine office without necessarily affirming the charism of papal infallibility, even when that charism is restricted by the various conditions imposed by Vatican I. The Church throughout most of its life was precisely in that situation, i.e., it functioned as the Body of Christ without reference to the infallibility of the pope.*

"Catholic theologians engaged in ecumenical dialogue, while standing fast by the teaching of the Church and searching together with separated brethren into the divine mysteries, should act with love for truth, with charity, and with humility," the Decree on Ecumenism declares (n. 11). "When comparing doctrines, they should remember that in Catholic teaching these exists an order or 'hierarchy' of truths, since they vary in their relationship to the foundation of the Christian faith."

It is at least theologically certain now that union with the Holy See is not necessary for communion with the Body of Christ. The teaching of Pope Pius XII has been supplanted by that of Vatican II which acknowledges the Christian reality of various non-Catholic Churches and ecclesial communities. What binds Christians together in a single body is their common faith in Jesus of Nazareth as Lord, their love and veneration of Sacred Scripture as the Word of God, the sacraments of baptism and Eucharist, or Lord's Supper, a common way of life nourished by faith in Christ, a lively sense of justice and a true neighborly charity, and a common desire to cling to the Gospel of Jesus Christ as the source of Christian virtue.[37] Such men and women have been incorporated into Christ and "have a right to be honored by the title of Christian, and are properly regarded as brothers in the Lord. . . ."[38] Vatican II insists, however, that there are degrees of participation in the life of the Church, but the issue of degrees is of secondary importance, once it has been acknowledged that the Body of Christ is really larger than the Catholic Church alone, and once we can see that the whole Body of Christ, and not the Catholic Church alone, is the "one, true Church of Christ."

While it is clearly true that one can be a Christian without accepting the dogma of papal infallibility, it is not nearly so clear that one can be a Catholic under such circumstances. This is the question which, in my judgment, Küng did not confront directly enough, particularly in the *America* article where he describes his reasons for staying in the Church.

What is necessary for communion with the Catholic Church? What is it that makes Catholicism a distinctive tradition and community within the total Body of Christ? What is the key to Catholic identity?

Certainly not faith in Jesus as the Christ. All Christians affirm that. Certainly not reverence for Sacred Scripture as a normative witness of that faith. All Christians accept that. Certainly not the celebration of the sacraments of salvation. All Christians, in varying ways, celebrate these, especially baptism and the Lord's Supper. Certainly not the acceptance of the Gospel as the basis of human existence. All Christians accept that, at least in principle. Certainly not the acknowledgement of the presence of God in the world and of our common responsibility to render him worship. Not only do all Christians acknowledge this, but so, too, do people of all religious faiths.

The decisive issue is centered in the understanding and exercise of collegiality. For the Catholic, the Church is a communion of churches, a community of Eucharistic communities. Each local community (a parish, a diocese, etc.) has responsibility for the mission of the whole Church. In a real sense, the whole Church is present in every local expression thereof. ("This Church of Christ is truly present in all legitimate local congregations of the faithful which, united with their pastors, are themselves called churches in the New Testament." [39]) The ultimate principle of unity in every local community is the Spirit of Christ; the sacramental principle of unity is the Eucharist; the ministerial principle of unity is the overseer, the one who, by ordination, has accepted responsibility for official, and therefore accountable, leadership within a given Eucharistic community or clusters thereof, the one who must see to it that all of the charisms, gifts, and resources present in those communities are coordinated and integrated so that all might work effectively for the common mission of the whole Church and become thereby signs of the Kingdom's presence among men.[40]

Catholics believe that the collegial nature of the Body of Christ must be symbolized both sacramentally and officially for the sake of the mission. This affects the way Catholic communities organize themselves and relate themselves to other churches which are so organized, and this also affects the way that Catholics come to understand the Gospel of Jesus Christ and come to articulate that understanding in speech or in writing.

How we perceive and express the Gospel of Jesus Christ is at the root of the difference between Catholics and other Christians. As Hans Küng wrote on the eve of Vatican II in his celebrated book, *The Council, Reform, and Reunion,* the fundamental issue dividing Catholics from their brother Christians is that of ecclesiastical office, specifically the question of the authority held and exercised for the service of the whole Church by the college of bishops, with the pope at its center and head.

And this is not merely a question of external organization. On the contrary, one's idea of ecclesiastical office will determine one's understanding of the process by which a Christian comes to know the meaning of the Gospel and then puts that understanding into words.

Most Christians agree that we come to an understanding of the Gospel in several different ways and through several different sources: the Bible itself, the interpretations of the great Fathers of the Church, the documents of the early councils, the writings of the classic theologians of the past, and even some of the data offered by the various non-theological disciplines, not to mention the whole range of everyday human experience.

But Christians do not agree on the role and authority of the college of bishops, and, more specifically, on the meaning of the papal office. Non-Catholic Christians generally do not acknowledge that the college of bishops has an irreplaceable function in holding in balance the various factors which make it possible to understand and to express the Gospel; namely, Scripture, tradition, and contemporary Christian experience.

Unlike his brother and sister Christians, the Catholic accords antecedent attention and respect to the stated positions, past and present, of the Church's college of bishops, whether expressed collectively or through its spokesman, the bishop of Rome. That is to say, when the Catholic is trying to make up his mind about some matter that touches upon his understanding of the Gospel or upon its exercise in the ethical order, he will always give serious weight to the guidelines proposed by this official, collegial source.

There may be occasions, as in the recent controversy over *Humanae Vitae,* where, after examination of the teaching proposed by official sources, the Catholic will disagree with, or even resist, these guidelines. But this is always the exception rather than the rule. When the Catholic finds that he is constantly at odds with the stated positions of the Church's college of bishops, past and present, then he must reassess his initial acceptance of, and commitment to, the Catholic tradition as such. In other words, he must begin to ask himself: Why am I a Catholic?

The point is developed in a different way in two of Gregory Baum's recent books, *The Credibility of the Church Today*,[41] which was his reply to Charles Davis, and *Faith and Doctrine*.[42] He argues that the Catholic Church alone offers the possibility of creating a doctrinal consensus on matters of faith and morals. It has an understanding of postbiblical tradition unlike that of any other Christian Church. Because of its distinctive self-understanding, the Catholic Church is best able to preserve the delicate balance between the past and the present, between the classic expressions of faith, including the biblical, and the application of the Gospel to modern times and conditions.

"The Catholic Church believes that the process of formulating doctrine, which the Spirit produced in the past, continues to go on in the present," he writes. "The divine tradition alive in the Church today enabled the Catholic Church to reinterpret her doctrinal position at Vatican II and renders her capable of continuing this in the future." [43]

Baum tends to claim too much in his apologetical argument on behalf of the Catholic Church, but at least he is conducting the argument at the right place, i.e., in the area of doctrinal formulation. Charles Davis, from an entirely different perspective, substantiates this view. In his *Question of Conscience* he, too, identifies the collegial structure of the Church as the distinctively Catholic feature of the Body of Christ, and he rejects Catholicism precisely at that point. For him the teaching authority and unifying function of the college of bishops, including the pope, have lost their claim to credibility.

Chapter II of the Dogmatic Constitution on Divine Revelation is a matter of some relevance here because it raises the same question. On the one hand, the chapter goes beyond some of the earlier and more rigid notions of Tradition, which tended to view Tradition as something totally independent of, and almost superior to, the testimony of Sacred Scripture. Scripture and Tradition were generally regarded by Catholics as two separate sources of revelation. Vatican II did not reaffirm this opinion. On the contrary, it left the question open. This was, in itself, a major ecumenical advance.

But the same chapter continues to insist upon the distinctively Catholic idea that the college of bishops plays an indispensable role in our understanding and expression of the Gospel. The frequently inept exercise of this magisterial office in our day should not be allowed to obscure this fundamental principle. Nowhere, however, does this fundamental principle seem to require infallibility, in such wise that the whole collegial construct would collapse without it. Catholics affirm the place of the college of bishops, including the one who fulfills the Petrine function of strengthening the faith of the brethren.[44] They are alone in this particular affirmation. It is a view that is, in the present ecumenical situation, distinctively Catholic.

It would indeed be very difficult to argue that one could reject the collegial principle as applied to the episcopacy and the papacy and still remain faithful to Catholic tradition. I am suggesting here—saying explicitly what Küng left unsaid—that affirmation of papal infallibility (or the infallibility of the Bible, or of ecumenical councils, or whatever) is not essential to the Catholic understanding of the Church. As a matter of historical record, the Body of Christ, and the Catholic sector thereof, functioned very well without reference to it throughout most of its lifetime, and its sudden breakthrough into the consciousness of the Catholic Church at Vatican I was dubious and precipitous.

Thesis #8: *Hans Küng is essentially right in his criticism of the traditional notion of papal infallibility and in reaffirming indefectibility as the basis of Christian fidelity to Christ and to his Gospel (or, more accurately, as the basis of God's fidelity to the Church). This position, as Küng himself suggests, has significant ecumenical possibilities.*

This last thesis is self-explanatory and serves as the conclusion of this essay.

I should predict that, just as we have seen remarkable

agreement among Catholic and non-Catholic Christian theologians on several important issues since Vatican II (I am thinking particularly of the agreement reached by the Catholic-Lutheran dialogue committee on such questions as the Real Presence, the Mass as a sacrifice, and ordained ministry), so, too, will the problem of papacy fall by the wayside as a barrier to ecumenical union.

"After the idea of episcopacy has been purged of its authoritarian elements, there remains a representative office," writes the Lutheran theologian, Wolfhart Pannenberg. "This important office represents not only the unity of the community as a whole, but also its connection with the Christian tradition in its development from the beginning and through all times. The same perspective applies to the papacy. It can be viewed as the highest office, representing not only the whole of present Christianity, but also its unity with the Church of the past. The papacy may have a significant and positive role in our active concern for Christian unity. . . . It is encouraging to note that many in the Roman Catholic Church are also reconsidering the role of the papacy, with a view toward its positive contribution to Christian unity. . . . It is possible to foresee a further stage in that process that would allow us to acknowledge the significance of a unified representation of Christianity." [45]

I salute Hans Küng for the contributions he has already made to theology, and specifically to ecclesiology, through his books, articles, and editorial work. I salute him for his latest book as well, my criticisms and reservations notwithstanding.

NOTES

1. All page references in this section are to *Infallible? An Inquiry*, unless otherwise indicated.
2. "The Theological Issues," *America* 124 (April 24, 1971) 428.
3. *Structures of the Church*, tr. S. Attanasio, New York: Nelson, 1964, p. 369.
4. *Ibid.*, p. 375.
5. *The Church*, tr. R. and R. Ockenden, New York: Sheed & Ward, 1967, p. 449.

6. *Ibid.*, p. 450.
7. *Art. cit.*, p. 427.
8. See Robert McAfee Brown's comment in *An American Dialogue* (with Gustave Weigel), New York: Doubleday, 1960, p. 30: "Far better that each partner recognize at the start that no amount of emphasis upon points held in common will dissipate the differences which still remain. There is no halfway house, for example, between believing (a) that the pope is infallible, and (b) that the pope is not infallible. Not even the combined genius of Catholic and Protestant theology could produce a satisfactory middle term; there is no such thing as being 'a little bit infallible'."
9. *America* 124 (March 20, 1971) 281-283.
10. *Structures of the Church*, p. 381.
11. "Documentation: Cardinal vs. Theologian," *The Month* (April, 1971) 106.
12. *Sacrae Theologiae Summa, vol. I: Theologia Fundamentalis*, Madrid: Biblioteca de Autores Cristianos, 1962 (5th ed.), pp. 700-701.
13. *Ibid.*, pp. 720-724.
14. *L'infaillibilité pontificale: source-conditions-limites*, Gembloux: Duculot, 1969, pp. viii and 176-182.
15. See, for example, J. Beumer, "Sind päpstliche Enzykliken unfehlbar?" *Theologie und Glaube* 42 (1952) 262-269; B. Brinkmann, "Gibt es unfehlbar Ausserungen des 'Magisterium ordinarium' des Papstes?" *Scholastik* 18 (1953) 202-221; H. Stirnimann, "Magisterio enim ordinario haec docentur," *Freiburger Zeitschrift für Philosophie und Theologie* I (1954) 17-47.
16. "Infaillibilité et indefectibilité," *Revue des sciences philosophiques et theologiques* 54 (1970) 607-608. For a carefully nuanced theological synthesis of the problem of papal infallibility, see the article "Infallibility," by H. Fries and J. Finsterhölzl *in Sacramentum Mundi*, vol. III, New York: Herder & Herder, 1969, pp. 132-138. See also K. Rahner's brief exegesis of the famous article 25 of the Dogmatic Constitution on the Church in *Commentary on the Documents of Vatican II*, vol. I, ed. H. Vorgrimler, New York: Herder & Herder, 1967, pp. 208-216.
17. *Op. cit.*, pp. 665-682.
18. *Ibid.*, p. 688.
19. *Ibid.*, pp. 688-689. These biblical arguments seem to betray an almost fundamentalistic interpretation of Sacred Scripture. For a refutation of these biblical arguments, on the same fundamentalistic grounds, see Bishop F. Simons' book, *Infallibility and the Evidence*, Springfield, Ill.: Templegate, 1968. See also

Bishop Simons' letter to *Commonweal* 94 (May 28, 1971) 295, wherein he defends his fundamentalistic method, on tactical grounds, against the passing criticism by Charles Davis in the latter's review of Küng's book in *Commonweal*, 93 (February 5, 1971) 447.

20. See, for example, my own survey of recent literature on the mission of the Church in *Church: The Continuing Quest*, New York: Newman Press, 1970.

21. See note #16 above.

22. *Art. cit.*, (note #16 above), p. 602, n. 4.

23. *Art. cit.* (note #16 above), p. 133.

24. *L'Eglise de saint Augustine*. . . , Paris: Cerf, 1970, pp. 244-248 and 385-389.

25. See Küng, *Structures of the Church*, pp. 9-27.

26. The change of the verb form in article 8 of the Dogmatic Constitution on the Church is of utmost significance here. Vatican II did not choose to reaffirm the teaching of Pope Pius XII in *Humani Generis*, namely that the Catholic Church and the Body of Christ are one and the same reality, in such wise that only Catholics are *real* members of the Church. Instead the council taught that the Body of Christ "subsists in" (rather than "is") the Roman Catholic Church. This formulation allows for the possibility of other churches' being in the Body of Christ, albeit with varying degrees of participation. This judgment seems to be confirmed by the Decree on Ecumenism, e.g., n. 20-23. See my earlier discussion of this question in *Do We Need the Church?*, New York: Harper & Row, 1969, pp. 141-145.

27. *Structures of the Church*, p. 39.

28. Vatican II's reaffirmation of Vatican I's teaching does not really alter the case. Vatican II may indeed have been more ecumenical than Vatican I, but this is a matter of degree, not of kind. Furthermore, Vatican II was unable to provide any additional intrinsic arguments on behalf of papal infallibility.

29. *Gaudium et Spes*, n. 81.

30. *A Question of Conscience*, New York: Harper & Row, 1967, p. 161. For my discussion of Davis' views, see *Do We Need the Church?*, pp. 186-188.

31. For a further discussion of this and other related points, see my book, *Who is a Catholic?*, Denville, N.J.: Dimension Books, 1971.

32. See pp. 353-366, especially p. 361 where Küng writes: "The definition of a pope signifies only an authoritative bearing of witness to the revelation that has occurred. . . ."

33. See R. Bultmann, "The Concept of Revelation in the New Testament," in *Existence and Faith*, London: Hoder & Stough-

ton, 1961, pp. 58-91; G. Moran, *Theology of Revelation*, New York: Herder & Herder, 1966; J. Moltmann, *Theology of Hope*, New York: Harper & Row, 1967. For a recent survey of the field, see A. Dulles, *Revelation Theology*. New York: Herder & Herder, 1969.

34. See *Infallible?*, Chapter IV.
35. *L'Eglise de saint Augustin. . .* , p. 248. Küng cites this same passage on p. 184.
36. *Art. cit.* (see note #16 above), pp. 615-618.
37. Decree on Ecumenism, n. 20-23.
38. *Ibid.*, n. 3.
39. Dogmatic Constitution on the Church, n. 17.
40. See the Dogmatic Constitution on the Church, n. 30, and the Decree on the Bishops' Pastoral Office in the Church, n. 17.
41. New York: Herder & Herder, 1968.
42. New York: Newman Press, 1969.
43. *The Credibility of the Church Today*, p. 146. See also *Faith and Doctrine*, pp. 95-98.
44. For a recent positive evaluation of the Petrine office, see *Papal Ministry in the Church* (*Concilium* series, vol. 64), ed. H. Küng, New York: Herder & Herder, 1971, and especially the brief essay by one of Küng's assistants, H. Häring, pp. 139-146.
45. *Theology and the Kingdom of God*, Philadelphia: Westminster Press, 1969, pp. 99-100.

Harry J.
McSORLEY

". . . [E]ven if a council errs in matters of faith, even if a pope errs in matters of faith, the church—through God's abundant grace in the Holy Spirit—nevertheless continues to exist permanently in Christ and remains nevertheless in his truth. . . . The continuity and indestructibility of the church . . . do not depend upon the infallibility of certain propositions but upon the Spirit, who works through the frailty and fallibility of men and their propositions. . . ." These thoughts, expressed almost a decade ago by Hans Küng in his first important book on ecclesiology,[1] are substantially reproduced in his new book on infallibility—but with a significant difference. In *Structures of the Church* Küng attributes these ideas to Protestants: to Luther, Calvin and Karl Barth.[2] In *Infallible? An Inquiry* [3] he makes the Protestant position his own.

The appropriation by Catholics of traditionally "Protestant" positions or emphases is, in itself, neither illegitimate nor surprising in view of the fact that Catholics and Protestants share much common Christian ground. One thinks of the reintroduction of the vernacular into the liturgy or the affirmation by the Second Vatican Council of the priesthood of all Christians and the necessity of the continual reformation of the church. Catholics who do not like to interpret these developments as a protestantizing of Catholicism might well argue that these changes are really not an embrace of Protestant practices and doctrines at all, but simply a return to an earlier stage of Catholic tradition. In either interpretation what makes Küng's new book so sensational is that he not only embraces a Protestant conception of infallibility (as we shall note, he actually goes beyond Luther and Calvin), but also proposes that Catholics reject the dogma of papal infallibility as defined by the First and as reaffirmed by the Second Vatican Council.[4]

Popular news media have already reported the sharp attack on Küng's position by Karl Rahner, Küng's lengthy and even sharper reply,[5] as well as the statements issued by the German, Italian and French hierarchies. Because the Rahner-Küng controversy deserves a separate evaluation in its own right I shall refer to it in this article only insofar as it elucidates our critical understanding of Küng's thesis on infallibility. One is forced to note with regret, however, the *ad hominem* character of much of Küng's response, a response which unnecessarily and, at times, unfairly calls into question the quality of Rahner's theological achievement. In fairness to Küng it must be acknowledged that Rahner was perhaps unnecessarily provocative when he suggested that Küng's method of argument as well as his basic thesis prevents the discussion from being "an inner-Catholic controversy".[6]

The Problem of Basic Methodology and the Question of Küng's Catholicity

Whether John McKenzie is correct in calling Rahner's judgment of Küng "extremely harsh" depends upon the way one interprets Küng's book as a whole. McKenzie takes Küng's book seriously for what it claims to be: a legitimate inquiry by a Catholic theologian who merely wants to open a discussion. For Rahner, the book is not simply an inquiry. He realizes, of course, that Küng intends it to be taken this way, but he insists that Küng's intention in no way neutralizes the fact that, throughout the book, Küng "denies something which, until now, has been an indisputable presupposition for an inner-Catholic discussion".[7]

Rahner returns to this point in his second response to

Küng when he asserts that there is a serious theoretical and methodological difference between Küng and himself. This emerges, says Rahner, when Küng claims that Rahner and other Catholic theologians have the burden of demonstrating from Scripture and from the history of the early church that the church has been promised propositional infallibility by Christ. Rahner grants that this is true when a Catholic theologian is using what has been called the method of fundamental theology, a method oriented primarily to those who do not share Catholic doctrinal presuppositions. However, by not accepting a dogma of the church until this kind of fundamental-theological "proof" is present, argues Rahner, Küng indicates that his standpoint is not really Catholic. If Küng stood within the Catholic theological community he would, with other Catholic theologians, continues Rahner, be open to the method of dogmatic theology. In this method of theologizing the actual faith-consciousness of the church is itself a decisive argument for the acceptance of a doctrine. Such a faith-consciousness concerning the ability of the church, under certain circumstances, to speak infallibly through the universal episcopate, through general councils and through popes, has been articulated at Vatican I and Vatican II. A theologian who did not accept this expression of the Catholic faith-consciousness, Rahner contends, would not really be a Catholic theologian.[8]

Küng's invocation, at the beginning and end of his book, of St. Augustine's classic statement of theological open-mindedness in his *De Trinitate* serves only to sharpen the methodological question. Augustine does ask his readers to keep an open mind when they share his hesitations about the doctrine of the Trinity and to correct him if he makes mistakes in his exposition of that doctrine. But the context of Augustine's declaration is not the same as Küng's. His work on the Trinity is intended both for believing Catholics who, like himself, have difficulties and for those others who consider it beneath their dignity to begin with faith and who are led into error by their perverse love of reason.[9] There are two significant things to note about Augustine's method in *De Trinitate:*

(1) He does not solve the difficulties he and others have

concerning the Trinity by denying the dogma, but by trying to explain the dogma in such a way that the "garrulous disputants . . . may return to the principles of faith and to the right course, and may at last realize how wholesome is the medicine that has been entrusted to the holy Church for the faithful".[10]

(2) Augustine realizes that his presentation of the dogma of the Trinity might be faulty and he therefore invites others to show him where he is wrong. But at no time does he call into question or challenge the Nicene dogma itself. In fact, for Augustine, this creed of the church, along with the Roman-Milan, African and pseudo-Athanasian creeds, is the "right rule of faith".[11] Augustine states that the Catholic interpreters of Scripture who have gone before him have taught, in accordance with Scripture, the doctrine of the Trinity that is expressed in the several creeds.[12] This Trinitarian faith of Scripture and of the creeds, he affirms, "is my faith, since it is the Catholic faith".[13]

In the light of these two observations about Augustine's theological method one might ask: doesn't Küng appeal to only one aspect of Augustine's method, that of openness to correction? Does he fully follow Augustine's "Catholic" methodology, namely, to the point of accepting not only the Catholic creeds as the rule of faith but also the decisions of plenary councils as *settlements* of previously disputed matters of faith? [14] By calling for the abandonment of the Vatican I definition of papal infallibility does not Küng depart from the method of Augustine and of all later Catholic theologians? At first glance it would seem so.

One must, however, be cautious here. Küng still insists that, in crisis situations, the church—through its councils —can and ought to speak in a "definitive", "obligatory", "dogmatic" and "binding" way. He even makes the important concession that councils can express the infallibility of the whole church.[15] And although Küng's church-oriented starting point is not adequately expressed in *Infallible?*, it does come across very clearly in a recent profession of his Catholicism when he says: "Like other Christians, I did not receive my Christianity from books, not even from the Bible. I received my Christianity from this community of faith, which has managed to make it through these last 2,000 years; which, time and again, one way or another, has managed to call forth faith in Jesus Christ and involvement in His spirit." [16]

It would seem, then, that one cannot put Küng outside the Catholic theological community simply by evaluating his theological method. This purely formal approach overlooks the evident sincerity with which Küng states at the beginning of *Infallible?*: ". . . [L]et it be known that the writer of this book is and remains for all his criticism a convinced Catholic theologian . . . deeply bound to his Church. . . ." (26). Perhaps it would be fairer to say that there seems to be a discrepancy in the theology Küng articulates and the Catholicism he professes. This appears to be the line of approach taken by the German bishops.[17]

Unclarity Surrounding Küng's Basic Thesis

A further observation is in order when discussing Küng's Catholicity. It concerns the formulation and the actual meaning of his basic thesis. What is this fundamental thesis? It is by no means easy to determine. This is one of the main faults of the book and is surely one of the main reasons Rahner was able to attack him so vigorously. I have found at least four different statements of Küng's basic position:

(1) "No one is infallible except God himself" (239-240).

(2) Neither Scripture, church, council nor pope is infallible "in the strict sense" (218-219).

(3) "[I]t has not been proved that faith is dependent on infallible propositions" (150).

(4) "The existence of propositions which are infallible in principle has not been convincingly substantiated either by Vatican I or Vatican II . . . [n]or is neoscholastic textbook theology able to demonstrate from the testimonies of Scripture and the testimonies of the oldest ecumenical tradition the necessity . . . or even merely the possibility, of propositions which must be a priori infallible" (151).

In my opinion it would be possible for a Catholic theologian to defend all four of these propositions without *ipso facto* ceasing to be Catholic. The most difficult to reconcile with the definition made by Vatican I is, of course, the first version of Küng's thesis. But if this thesis is understood in terms of Küng's second proposition, where the operative phrase is "in the strict sense", and if Küng were to affirm that there is a broad or loose sense in which Scripture, church, council and pope can, under certain conditions, be said to be infallible,[18] then both versions (1) and (2) of his thesis are readily reconcilable with the teaching of Vatican I. As Bishop Gasser's official exposition of the infallibility dogma makes clear, the pope's infallibility is "in no sense . . . absolute, because absolute infallibility belongs to God alone".[19] Here, at least, Küng and Vatican I are in clear agreement.

The difficulty arises when Vatican I goes on to define that the pope shares the infallibility (in the broad, non-absolute, therefore, limited and conditioned sense) of the whole church. Here Küng does not clearly affirm what Vatican I clearly affirms. This is surely one of the reasons for the statement by the German bishops that Küng's book does not uphold "several fundamental elements of the Catholic understanding of faith and the church".[20] Küng does not say Vatican I was wrong, but that it was blind to the basic problematic of infallible propositions (152).[21] Küng points out quite rightly in his reply to Rahner that: "If a council did not see something as a problem, it has not decided it." [22] But he overlooks the obvious counter-question: what about the problem that Vatican I did see and did decide? [23]

It does not really seem, however, that Küng's main thesis, the one he will stand by and not simply set forth as an hypothesis, is that Vatican I was blind to the linguistic problems connected with infallible propositions. Both in his response to Rahner [24] and in a recent interview [25] he indicates that versions (3) and (4) of his basic thesis are the ones that he is really sure of. If this is so, then it is even easier to "save" Küng's Catholicity. For, to absolutely reject the Vatican I dogma is one thing. Not to uphold it or defend it is another thing. And to say that this dogma has *not been proved* is still another thing. If, according to P. Fransen,[26] the "first rule" for the interpreting of conciliar texts is that only the central assertion in a decree or canon is defined, and all the rational, biblical and dogmatic arguments put forward to support the central assertion "are not final, . . . may be corrected and even, with certain limits, be called into question", then Küng's demand for more "proof" or "convincing arguments" can readily be reconciled with Catholic Christianity. However, if Küng's main thesis were: "Unless I have been given convincing proof, I will not accept the Vatican I dogma," then perhaps Rahner would be justified in calling this an attitude that is no longer Catholic, for it would mean that Küng, contrary to his assertion quoted above,[27] does not really receive his Christianity from the Catholic Church. As we indicated at the beginning of this paragraph, however, this does not seem to be the thesis Küng really wants to defend.

Observations on Küng's Demand for "Proof"

Küng's assertion that Catholic theology has yet to provide convincing proof for the dogma of papal infallibility or even for the possibility of infallible propositions can express the legitimate concern of a critical theologian. But because Küng again and again [28] demands "proof"—either from the bible (198-199) or from the bible and the "oldest ecumenical tradition" (151)—because he seems to place such stress on the fundamental-theological task, then the question of theological method is raised once again and some critical observations are in order. As Rahner explains in an important passage of his "Replik", there seems to be an essential difference between Küng and traditional Catholic theology "in the interpretation of the normative significance of the actual faith-consciousness of the Church as this is expressed in its dogmas. Naturally Küng can demand that this self-understanding of the Catholic Church and its magisterium be also demonstrated in a fundamental-theological way and not be dealt with by me only as a presupposition of an inner-Catholic dogmatic dialogue. In relation to the controversy with Küng, however, I certainly do not have to address myself to this fundamental-theological task. To fulfill this task is surely difficult. But before one utilizes this difficulty he should, both as a Christian and as a theologian, be clear about the fact that the task of proving in a fundamental-theological way the absolutely normative significance of Jesus Christ is more or less just as difficult".[29]

One wonders if Küng's constant demand for "proof" does not betray some of the very rationalism that he abhors in the 19th century Catholicism that defined the dogma of infallibility.[30] Küng does distinguish "the clarity of rationality" from the "pseudo-clarity of rationalism" (168) and he surely wants his theology and his faith to be characterized by the former. But if Küng's main thesis is what I think it is, namely, that there is no "proof" for the Vatican I dogma, is it not necessary to point out with even the older manuals of apologetics that, although there are indeed rational and historical grounds for what Christians believe (and it is the task of apologetics and fundamental theology to supply those grounds), no one ever becomes a Christian or remains a Christian simply because the divine authority of Jesus Christ or the other dogmas of the church have been "proved" to him in the sense that these would become evident and compelling to the mind solely on the basis of the "proofs" adduced? Illuminating grace is always necessary for one to believe *in* Christ or to believe *that* Christ was raised from the dead and *that* he will come again in judgment. One may well ask further if the term "proof" really has anything to do with the faith of Christians who no longer are able to put their hands into the wounds of their risen Lord. Is it not much better to speak of scriptural "indications" rather than "proofs" for a Christian dogma? Even in the older apologetics one did not "prove" a dogma in the strict sense; one simply proved or gave evidence that the dogma was believ*able*.[31]

What Richard McBrien has written concerning Charles Davis' demands for more proof of the church's credibility can be applied to Küng's thesis that no one has yet "proved" papal infallibility: His "demands for the signs of credibility seem too absolute. . . . The signs of credibility will always be ambiguous.

They are usually such as neither to command assent nor render their rejection inevitable. [H]e has read these signs one way . . . , but men of equal integrity and theological competence have continued to read them in another. . . . The evidence from the Bible and from history is neither so clear as to compel assent, nor so weak as to undercut entirely the distinctively Catholic commitment".[32]

Küng dissociates himself from those opinions of Bishop Francis Simons [33] which he judges are too influenced by a "neo-scholastic fundamental theology". Yet he agrees "with his main thesis that the infallibility of the ecclesiastical teaching office must be proved from Scripture to be acceptable, but plainly cannot be proved" (198-199). What kind of scriptural "proof" would Küng accept, especially in view of his thesis that not even the propositions of Scripture are inerrant (219-220)? To whom is this "proof" to be directed? Can we "prove" the absolute significance of Jesus to non-Christians from the bible? Can Küng "prove" to Oscar Cullmann from Scripture that Christ intended the ministry of Peter to continue in his successors? If not, does this mean that neither he nor other Catholics have a sound basis for believing that such a ministry was in some way intended by Christ for his church? Could Küng prove to an Anabaptist from Scripture that infant baptism is a good and legitimate practice? Luther couldn't. In fact, he rejected the Anabaptist demand for clear biblical proof, pointing out that there was an implicit biblical argument that became probative when taken in the light of the practice of the universal church.[34] It would seem that Küng's method of argumentation would be more at home in a dialogue with the Anabaptists than with the Lutherans. With reference to the doctrine of the Virgin Birth, Luther did not say he would only accept it if someone proved it to him. Rather, since it was part of the creed, he argued, one should profess it. Besides, he adds, it has stood for a long time "without being *disproved*".[35]

In *The Church* Küng rightly pointed out that "there is one thing that Orthodox and Protestant theologians . . . cannot dispute: the ministerial primacy of a single person is not contrary to Scripture".[36] (Cannot the same be said of a properly qualified

infallibility of such a minister?) In saying this Küng has laid an
important foundation for an ecumenical dialogue on the papacy. It is regrettable that he did not follow up this possibly
fruitful line of thinking in his present inquiry. For Luther "does
not demand that the validity of every doctrine and practice be
established by an explicit command of Scripture".[37] All that is
required is that the doctrine attested by the consent of the
whole church not be contradictory to Scripture but be in ac-
cord and harmony with it.[38]

General Evaluation of *Infallible?*

It is impossible to give a complete evaluation of Küng's
book in this article. Even though it is a relatively short work, it
contains scores of exegetical, historical, philosophical and sys-
tematic-theological judgments, many of which could evoke a
lengthy critical analysis. For this reason I will simply make two
overall observations, one positive and one negative, and then
proceed to some of the more important specific points that call
for criticism.

The first thing that ought to be said in evaluating this
book as a whole, having considered the formal questions of
basic theological methodology and burden of proof, is that it is
an important book dealing with an important theme, a theme
that is just beginning to get the attention it deserves in the
various national and international ecumenical-theological conversations. The book is written with the courageousness and
the rhetorical power that have characterized nearly all of
Küng's work. One will find a great deal of truth in this book,
uttered, at times, with prophetic forcefulness (I think especially
of pp. 222-247). Above all, this book will compel Catholic
theologians to address themselves to a thorough rethinking
and restatement of the doctrine of infallibility in a manner
that will make sense not only to separated Christians but to
questioning Catholics as well.

The second general evaluation one must make of this
book, however, is that, in comparison with the quality of

Küng's three previous major theological works (we leave aside his still untranslated work on Hegel and think only of *Justification, Structures* and *The Church*), this book ranks a poor fourth. It does not approximate any of the other three in carefulness of argument, depth of research or sympathetic use of related historical and systematic studies done by other Catholic —or even Protestant—theologians.[39]

Specific Criticisms

1. *Old Premises, New Conclusion:* Küng's inquiry into the problem of infallibility did not begin in the present book. It was well underway both in *Structures* [40] and in *The Church*,[41] works to which Küng frequently refers to support the argument of *Infallible?* Indeed, there is practically no theological insight or piece of evidence in *Infallible?* that cannot be found, at least in incipient form, in either of the two previous ecclesiological works, including, as we shall see, his linguistic-philosophical argument.

What makes *Infallible?* so different from the earlier books is that its *conclusion* is so different, even though the premises, the materials from which the different conclusion is drawn, are still basically the same!

In 1964, for example, expressing the same insight that can later be found in *The Church*,[42] Küng could write: ". . . [P]erhaps the day will come when it will be fully realized that although the term 'infallibility' does indeed express the binding force of the formulations of the faith, it does not indicate their binding character. With this in mind perhaps a concept will then be found which, better than the term 'infallibility', will present in an encompassing and balanced manner the strict binding force of decrees *and* at the same time their profoundly incomplete character—retaining the respectively true and permanent content of both elements." [43]

In the present book Küng proposes that, instead of saying the church's confessions of faith or conciliar and papal definitions are infallible, we should simply say that the whole church

will abide in the truth of Christ even though the binding definitions of the truth of Christ by councils and popes can be erroneous. Küng's new proposal indeed expresses clearly the
fragmentary and the provisional aspect of the church's formulations of faith. But his refusal to admit that conciliar and papal
decisions can be infallible [44] leads to the most unsatisfactory
conclusion that the church's official teaching ministry can
definitively be teaching something *heretical* which is "binding"
on the whole church! Küng grants that there can be "confessing
situations", for example, that of the church in Nazi Germany,
where the church has to speak "a definitive Yes or No" (148).
But even here, on the basis of Küng's theory that there can be
no propositional infallibility, it is possible for the confessing
church to be wrong in the path it defines and obliges the
Christian people to follow. His new approach, then, does preserve the fragmentary aspect of faith formulations, but it
hardly gives a satisfactory· explanation of the "binding force"
of such formulations. He thus is working with the same data
that he had in 1964 and 1967, but reaches quite a different
conclusion than he did previously. He once tried to balance
the two aspects of the fragmentariness and the bindingness of
church definitions; now he asserts, without introducing new
evidence, that "fragmentary" can mean "erroneous" and, by
implication, that these definitions are "binding" and "definitive"
even though they may be erroneous.

2. *Humanae Vitae: A New Factor But a Bad Starting
Point:* The one really new dimension that is operative in
Infallible?, in contrast to Küng's earlier work, is his strong
feeling of frustration because of the "relapse" by the Roman
Curia and Pope Paul "into . . . preconciliar absolutism, juri-
dicism, and centralism" (19). What he means by this is detailed more than candidly in his "A Candid Preface" (11-30).
This relapse, Küng contends, is nowhere better illustrated than
in Pope Paul's encyclical on family limitation, *Humanae Vitae.*
The entire first chapter of the book is devoted to an examination
of this encyclical (31-63).

I am in complete agreement with Küng that *Humanae*

Vitae has had as one of its unintended consequences a massive "examination of conscience" about the meaning of the teaching authority in the Catholic Church (33). I agree only partly with him, however, when he says this encyclical "is extraordinarily revealing in regard to the problem of infallibility" (33). It is extraordinarily revealing not, as Küng thinks, because it tells us something about what infallibility *is* and the harm it can cause, but because it reveals to both Protestants and Catholics what infallibility *is not*.

It has had such a clarifying effect for Protestants as to what infallibility does not mean that Robert McAfee Brown could write: *"Humanae Vitae* is . . . inadvertently the greatest gift to the ecumenical scene since the election of Pope John. . . . For its reception shows conclusively that traditional views of papal authority simply cannot be taken seriously any more, and that Catholics feel no greater sense of being bound to unquestionable doctrine than do Protestants. . . . With one stroke of the pen, Pope Paul has cut through and resolved the most vexing ecumenical problem of all. . . ." [45]

Humanae Vitae has also been extraordinarily revealing to Catholics because so many of them became aware for the first time that their understanding of papal infallibility was much too exaggerated. From statements of national episcopal conferences, from individual theologians of great stature, including Rahner, and from groups of theologians they learned that not everything the pope teaches in an encyclical is infallible or demands unquestioning assent—not even when the encyclical is addressed to the whole church and concerns a question of "morals" [46] and is a reaffirmation of previous papal teaching. Catholics further learned from the same sources that they could, in good conscience and without repudiating their status as church members, dissent from the encyclical teaching if they had serious reasons for not accepting it. [47]

Both for Catholics and Protestants *Humanae Vitae* was extraordinarily revealing about the problem of infallibility. But I do not agree with the reason for which Küng finds it revealing. For him, the minority group of "Roman" theologians on the papal advisory commission were perfectly correct in telling

Pope Paul that he *could not* change the teaching of his predecessors. For him, the Roman theologians were faithfully and logically interpreting Vatican I's teaching on papal infallibility when they argued that the papal and universal episcopal [48] prohibition of contraception was "factually infallible" (55-58). In the face of the arguments of the Roman theologians, says Küng, "There are only two possibilities: either, like the minority of the commission and the Pope, treat such teaching as infallible and irreversible and adhere to it despite all difficulties . . . ; OR simply question this whole theory of infallibility" (67-68).

Küng thus sets up a disastrously false dilemma: disastrous because it shapes the whole course of his book and locks him into a hostile attitude toward *any* concept of infallibility; [49] false because, aside from the handful of "Roman theologians" whom Küng is combating, it is hard to think of any theologians besides Küng or even of any national episcopal conferences—including those of the United States and Italy—who have received *Humanae Vitae* as an infallible document. They are all aware, as Küng was in *Structures,* that "*all* conditions without exception must be fulfilled and surely and solidly established before one can talk of an infallible definition. Hence the [Code of Canon Law] definitively states: 'Unless expressly stated no matter is held as declared or dogmatically defined' ".[50] If Küng has the consensus of Catholic theologians with him in holding that *Humanae Vitae* is erroneous in its condemnation of certain forms of contraception, he surely has the consensus of theologians against him when he holds that it is, in terms of the teaching of Vatican I, infallible.

It is not surprising that Rahner vigorously attacks Küng on this point.[51] Taking a stance similar to that of Newman a century ago, Rahner states: "Even if the minority commission had said that this question calls for an absolutely definitive assent, this would have been only the opinion of this minority and nothing more." [52] In his response, Küng agrees with Rahner's surmise [53] that he really doesn't place a decisive value on the argument that *Humanae Vitae* is to be taken as infallible.[54] He still insists that, according to the principles of "Roman theology" (which he strangely seems to equate with Roman Catholic theology or with the teaching of Vatican I), *Humanae Vitae* is infallible, but allows that one can hold an opposite opinion without overthrowing his basic thesis: "There is no theological proof for a priori infallible propositions by the official leaders of the church." Küng says he chose the *Humanae Vitae* example because it demonstrates "a regrettable consequence of a false conception of the magisterium of the church". He says he could have begun his inquiry with "the question of Pope Honorius, or the condemnation of religious freedom or . . . any other of the . . . errors of the church's magisterium".[55]

I wish to make two comments on Küng's use of *Humanae Vitae* as the starting point of his inquiry. First, one might well argue that Pope Paul's conviction that he had to maintain the teaching of his predecessors concerning contraception was based much more on an exaggerated and, therefore, false conception of the magisterium of the church than on insight into the natural law. But this argues *for* a critique of false conceptions of magisterium, not *against* the Vatican I doctrine of infallibility. Catholic theologians should indeed undertake to unmask harmful theological opinions concerning the magisterium or any other doctrine. These *opinions* or explanations of a doctrine are not to be confused or equated with the *binding doctrine* itself. This means, specifically, that in this important task of theological criticism it is necessary to make clear before all else that the opinion of theologians who wish to extend the object of papal, episcopal or ecclesial infallibility so as to include *every* question of natural law ethics is an opinion which has no foundation in the teaching of the First Vatican Council.[56]

Equally important for any theological critique that would correct some of the exaggerated theology of the magisterium still operative in influential circles [57] is a critical restatement of the Vatican I dogma itself, not only in terms of Vatican II's doctrine of collegiality, but also in terms of something of extraordinary importance that neither Vatican I nor Vatican II faced up to—and the contemporary church should feel indebted to Hans Küng for pointing this out both in *Structures* [58] and in the present work (107)—namely, the conflict situations between pope and church which have existed many times during the history of the church, not excluding the present, and which necessitate concrete *juridical* norms in addition to the usual *moral* exhortations in order to check tendencies either toward an exaggerated conciliarism or toward papal absolutism.

While granting to Küng, then, the necessity of a sound and massive theological criticism of any false conceptions of the magisterium of the church, I still do not see that this, of itself, necessitates a rejection of the doctrine of infallibility. Nor did Küng think so in *Structures*, even though he was aware at that time that a considerable and pernicious amount of the ultramontane maximizing of the papal office continued after Vatican I, notwithstanding the fact that Vatican I did not endorse such harmful misconceptions.

My second comment is that, by choosing *Humanae Vitae* as the starting point of his inquiry, Küng unnecessarily complicates, obfuscates and overheats an already difficult question. The very passion with which he writes his preface and his first chapter hardly contributes to the carefulness of procedure and argumentation that is required if one is to make a significant theological—as distinct from church-political—contribution on this important theme.

A serious ecumenical-theological inquiry into the problem of infallibility should *never* begin with the encyclical *Humanae Vitae!* In fact, it should not even begin with a discussion of *papal* infallibility. There is no sense discussing the doctrine of papal infallibility with other Christians if they do not hold to a doctrine of conciliar infallibility. And there is no sense discussing conciliar infallibility unless one has first agreed that there is a real sense in which the entire Christian church shares in the infallibility of the Holy Spirit of truth. On this point there is, happily, solid common ground shared by Catholic, Anglican, Orthodox, Lutheran [61] and Calvinist traditions—which is not to say there has been adequate theological reflection on this doctrine by theologians of those traditions, or that this doctrine has even been remembered by all contemporary theologians representing those traditions. [62]

With this criticism of Küng's method of approaching his subject I do not intend, as Rahner did to Küng's chagrin,[63] to tell Küng what he should have done or should do. I offer it simply as a critique of what he actually did and also as a proposal for future ecumenical research to which I myself hope to contribute.

3. *Küng's Exegesis of Vatican I and Vatican II:* In *Structures,* with one notable exception that will soon be pointed out, Küng's interpretation of Vatican I was admirably precise in contrast to what we find in the present book. In *Structures,* for example, Küng could write: "If we are not to fall victim to misunderstandings at the outset in this discussion, everything will depend upon an exact understanding of papal infallibility as it has been understood by Vatican I. All too often outside the Church the Vatican definition is considered . . . as the establishment of an unlimited papal infallibility. At the same time it is a fact that this very definition signifies a very clear *limitation vis-à-vis* all that which frequently had been asserted about the infallibility of the pope in the Catholic Church before the council. One could rightly view it as a victory for the council minority. . . . Compare . . . the formula proposed by Archbishop Manning with what was ultimately defined after the most heated discussions. Manning's formula spoke with a complete lack of differentiation of the infallibility of every papal pronouncement on matters of faith and morals. . . . But . . . the Council laid down very definite conditions against it which in fact very strongly limited the infallibility of the pope." [64]

What has happened since 1962 that enables Küng to assert now, with no indication that he has done any new research, that, for Vatican I, "the pope, of himself, at any time, without necessarily bringing in the Church or the episcopate, can claim ecclesiastical infallibility and with finality decide alone any question of theory or practice that is important for the Church" (101)? That this is a caricature of the Vatican I dogma, both in what it implies about the *separability* of the papal teaching ministry from the church and in its totally imprecise statement of the *object* of infallibility, can best be seen by reading what Küng himself has said about these matters in *Structures*.[65]

One place where Küng seriously misreads Vatican I, both in *Structures* (370 and 374) and in *Infallible?* (105), has to do with Bishop Gasser's explanation of the duty of the pope to consult with the bishops. Gasser states that the drafters of the text did not want to say that the pope has a strict or absolute obligation to consult with the *bishops* prior to making an infallible definition, even though this would be the "ordinary means" of procedure.[66] But in both books Küng misinterprets Gasser by attributing to him the view that the pope has no absolute duty to consult the *church*. Gasser does not explicitly state this absolute necessity of the pope to consult the church or the church's faith, but it is clear from a number of things in Gasser's exposition that this is the case. Two examples can be given here.

The first is that the "rule of faith even for papal definitions" is the *"consensio* of the churches". But because this *"consensio . . .* can be deduced from the clear and manifest testimonies of Sacred Scripture, from the *consensio* of antiquity . . . or from the teaching of theologians, or through other private ways which all suffice for full information . . . as to what the churches think"—because this is so, it is wrong to say the pope must consult the *bishops,* even though, Gasser adds, it is true that their *consensio* is also a rule of faith.[67] What is overlooked by Küng is that the pope *is* bound—and bound absolutely, even though Gasser does not use that word —to search out the faith of the whole *church* prior to making a definition of that faith.[68]

A second indication that Vatican I intended that the pope necessarily be bound to consult the faith of the church is that, when discussing the situation where there is doctrinal disagreement in the church, Gasser does not say: go to the pope and he will have the answer. Nor does he say recourse is to be had "to the mind of Rome" or "the mind of the pope". Rather, he says, recourse is to be had "to the *consensus* of antiquity, that is, to Scripture and to the holy fathers, and from the *consensio* of antiquity the dissent of present preaching is to be resolved".[69] Had Küng made use of this part of Gasser's exposition, he would not have said in *Structures* (374): "If the pope merely wills it, he can [make definitions] ultimately even without the Church." Nor would he have said in *Infallible?:* "The teaching of Vatican I really amounts to this: if he wants, the pope can do anything, even without the Church" (105). Much more faithful to both the spirit and the letter of Vatican I is George Tavard's thesis: "In his definitions, encyclicals, instructions and actions, [the pope] must embody the Church's unanimity, which is not reached by obedience to one man's opinions and decisions but by free and mutual consultation and discussion in the spirit of the Gospel. Papal encyclicals which do not embody this unanimity are theological documents with no claim on the allegiance of the Church's members." [70]

As for Küng's Vatican II exegesis, he is mistaken when he suggests that the recent council simply took over uncritically the Vatican I dogma of infallibility. Two examples will suffice to show that Vatican II clarified more than Vatican I the *limits* of infallibility.

The Vatican I definition states that the object of infallibility is "matters of faith and *mores*".[71] As we have shown in point 2 above, it was the intention of Vatican I that these "matters" be either revelation itself or truths intimately related to divine revelation. Moreover, the council did not think that *all* moral principles were so related to the deposit of faith that they could all be considered part of the object of the church's infallibility.[72] This must be said in opposition to Küng, who thinks that, according to both Vatican I and II, there is virtually no question that cannot pertain to the object of infallible authority (74). True, it is only by studying the Vatican I *acta*, especially Bishop Gasser's exposition, that one can discern Vatican I's intention to limit infallibility to revelation or to matters necessary for explaining and preserving that revelation. At Vatican II, however, such a clarification was explicitly made in the promulgated text itself where we read: "This infallibility . . . extends as far as the deposit of revelation extends. . . ." [73] When Küng suggests that the qualifying

phrase added to these words— ". . . which must be faithfully
expounded"—means that there is nothing that cannot be part
of the safeguarding of the faith and therefore nothing that
cannot be defined infallibly (74), he ignores the explanatory
relatio to this sentence, which states: "The object of the infallibility of the church, thus expounded, has the same extension as the revealed deposit; it therefore extends to all those
things and only to those things (*et ad ea tantum*) which
either directly touch upon the revealed deposit or which are
required for religiously guarding and faithfully explaining the
revealed deposit." [74] In the case of the papal teaching against
contraception, this would mean that such teaching could only
fall within the indirect object of the church's infallibility if it
were able to be shown that, unless this *particular* teaching were
maintained, some aspect of *revelation* pertaining to marriage
would no longer be able to be upheld. To my knowledge, no
recent moralist has even attempted to demonstrate this.

Another example indicating that Vatican II did not simply
parrot the Vatican I dogma concerns the anti-Gallican formula:
"ex sese, non ex consensu ecclesiae". Vatican II indeed repeated the formula of Vatican I, but it is not true to say, as
Küng does, that this phrase was simply and uncritically "ham-
mered in" (75). The formula was used at Vatican II only after
the theological commission pointed out, *in confrontation with
Pope Paul,* that a formula he had proposed was "excessively
simplified" and liable to "induce new anxiety" among many
bishops "especially concerning relations with Eastern Christians, as is clear from the history of that other formula: 'ex
sese et non ex consensu Ecclesiae' ".[75] It would seem, then,
that the most accurate thing that can be said about Vatican
II's use of the controversial and misleading formula of Vatican
I is that its misleading character was recognized and that it
was used with a strong reservation which indicated Vatican II's
awareness that much work remains to be done before a happier
formulation is achieved concerning the relationship between
the pope and the rest of the church.

Furthermore, the *relatio* attached to this dangerous formula points out something of extraordinary importance for

understanding the relationship between definitions of faith and the faith of the church. The *relatio* states that infallible definitions of a pope or of general councils "are irreformable of themselves, and do not require the approbation of the people, as many in the East erroneously hold, *but they carry with them and express the consensus of the whole community*".[76] The Vatican II theological commission thus gives a newer and clearer formulation of the intimate relationship between pope and church than Gasser's commission was able to achieve a century ago. Infallible definitions of pope or council, according to Vatican II, are simply expressions of the consensus of the church's faith. They are not and cannot be an imposition of something the Christian people does not believe. Hans Küng is simply wrong, therefore, when he says that, "for all those acquainted with the terminology [the *ex sese* formulation] quite clearly meant that, for the complete validity of an infallible definition by the pope, no consent of the Church—previously, simultaneously, or subsequently—is necessary. . . ." (102).[77]

4. *Is Infallibility "A Priori"?:* The Vatican II material just presented leads me to register a further critique of Küng's book. *In Structures* (378) and in *Infallible?* (147, 150, 151, 203, 206), as well as in his reply to Rahner,[78] Küng speaks of the Catholic doctrine of the "a priori" infallibility of councils and popes. This surely complicates the discussion by introducing an element that has no place in it and it raises the question as to whether Küng is jousting with a straw man. There are a number of reasons for insisting that the concept of infallibility is distorted by referring to it as "a priori" infallibility.

First of all, neither Vatican I nor Vatican II teaches that infallibility is "a priori". One does not even find this notion in the *relationes* of those councils, not to mention the promulgated texts.

Second, both Vatican I and Vatican II indicate clearly that the infallible faith of the church and the consensus of the church is *prior* to any infallible definition of that faith.[79]

Third, Hans Küng himself recognized in *Structures* that the existence of a faith-consensus in the church is always *prior* to any papal definition.[80]

Fourth, even according to Vatican I ecclesial infallibility is not to be considered as absolute; therefore it is conditional. Only *after* certain conditions have been fulfilled, among which is the searching out of the faith of the church—thus, only *a posteriori*—can there be any such thing as an infallible papal or conciliar definition.[81] Further, for such disparate theologians as Augustine and Robert Bellarmine, Christian *experience*—hence, something that is by definition *a posteriori*—is a necessary prelude to at least some new definitions of faith or mores.[82]

Fifth, but most importantly, the infallibility of the church, of councils or of popes is always *posterior* to the promise of the Lord to send his Holy Spirit of truth to the church.

Sixth, when the prior conditions are realized and a dogma is defined, it does have a prior claim on the Christian believer's assent in that it has a formal authority even before the individual Christian examines it. But this does not mean that the Christian is to accept the dogma blindly, uncritically or unreflectively. It is precisely on this point—concerning the reception of dogma—that Catholic theology has much work to do. And it is precisely on this point that John Calvin registered one of his central and most telling criticisms of what he took to be the contemporary Catholic understanding of the authority of councils.[83] Catholic theologians have been giving increasing attention to this problem. Rahner thinks Küng's book may well provide the impetus for a general theological rethinking of this and related problems.[84]

If a Catholic theologian wishes to work with traditional Lutheran terminology, he can say that dogmatic definitions of the faith of the whole church by popes or councils are a "norma normans" for the articulation of the faith of the believer. But Scripture can be regarded as a "norma normans, non normata"[85] for the faith of the church and for the official dogmatic norms articulated by the church. This means that dogmas "always have to be measured against Scripture".[86]

Rahner thinks he and Küng are in agreement up to this point, but differ concerning the question: how precisely is the justification of the church's magisterial statements in terms of Scripture to take place? Do these dogmatic pronouncements only possess a normative character for the Catholic theologian after he, by himself and according to his own estimation, deems this justification to be successful? Or do magisterial pronouncements have a degree of bindingness for him—different in each case—even before he has personally confronted the dogma with Scripture? [87]

It seems to me that not only Küng, but Calvin also, would agree that the teaching of a properly constituted council ought rightly to be considered as normative, at least in the sense of being a preliminary decision or a precedent (*praeiudicium*) for the Christian in articulating his faith.[88]

For one to have a Catholic attitude in this regard it would seem at least necessary that one not make an a priori reservation *against* the genuine dogmas of the church. Speaking positively, it would be essential to a Catholic attitude that one receive the dogma with an open mind and with the expectancy that it will be a helpful, life-expanding, fresh statement of the good news announced by Jesus Christ.

The definition of the Marian dogmas has, it is no secret, strained the readiness of many Catholics to see dogma as having anything to do with the fullness of life Jesus came to bring.[89] These "marginal dogmas" are so far removed from the "foundation of the Christian faith" [90] that it requires great theological ability to show what these dogmas have to do with salvation and with the mission of the church. A serious Catholic theologian should at least *presume* there is such a relationship and he should then set about trying to interpret the marginal dogma in the light of the fundamental evangelical message.

This attitude of openness toward whatever aspect of the foundational saving message is intended to be proclaimed by the new formulation of faith is, in this ecumenical age, not confined to Catholics. At the Boston College Conference on Vatican I (December, 1970), the Lutheran theologian, George

Lindbeck, was among the Protestant participants who said that ecumenicity forbids Protestants from saying "a priori that a doctrine stated by the Pope was irretrievably false; . . . there should be an effort to explore the truth which might be contained within such a pronouncement and which might conceivably be a restating of the Gospel revelation in modern categories".[91] Compare this attitude of ecumenically minded Protestants with that of John McKenzie, who says he has no problem confessing the dogmas of the Assumption and the Immaculate Conception because he has "not the slightest idea of what either dogma means".[92] Shouldn't a Catholic theologian at least presume that such dogmas have *some* Christian meaning, *some* "relationship to the foundation of the Christian faith"? Is it not his task to try to point out the meaning the dogma can have for the Christian life, especially when the magisterium has failed to do so? [93]

That there can be and has been default on the part of the magisterium in fulfilling its task of pointing out the *saving meaning* of dogmas cannot be denied.[94] Rahner has written with increasing directness to remind the magisterium of its "duty to examine whether a proposition, the definition of which is urged, really is so related to the substance of the faith that the ordinary believer can genuinely assent to this proposition from the ultimate depth of his Christian decision". One can demand this of the magisterium because "definitions must not be made solely as exercises of obedience toward the formal teaching authority".[95]

A final word on the question of "a priori" infallibility. In his response to Küng, Rahner says he does not think a Catholic theologian can make use of any "legal" or "logical" reservation (*Vorbehalt*) against a definition of the magisterium. The theologian, he says, in a sense gives the magisterium a "blank check".[96] I don't think this is at all a good way to formulate the relationship of the Christian to the magisterium. This manner of speaking does not incorporate Rahner's other, balancing assertions, which imply that there is *always* the reservation of one's free, conscientious decision, which is not made once and for all in accepting the Catholic "system", but must be made again and again—including, I would add, the moment of the promulgation of the dogma of the Assumption. There is, moreover, the reservation necessarily implied in the critical interpretation of dogma which Rahner stresses in a way that I think would please John Calvin.[97] These other assertions also explain why Rahner can say that, in his lifetime, he has never had to refuse assent to any of the dogmas—in the proper sense—of the Catholic Church, nor has he ever ceased to be a "free theologian".[98]

5. *Propositions, Truth and Infallibility:* We noted above, in our first point of specific criticism, that, already in his earlier work, Küng pointed out the linguistic-philosophical difficulties associated with propositions as such.[99] In the present work Küng develops his reflections on this problem by making use of five propositions (which he calls "points" or "observations" instead of propositions) about propositions drawn from the unpublished work of his student, J. Nolte (157-173).

Since Charles Davis has said that this section of the book "will seem elementary to those familiar with modern discussions of religious language",[100] it ought to be stated first of all that Küng himself admits that his presentation here is "brief" and that he explicitly says he is not making use of modern linguistic philosophy (157). His "very modest" aim is simply to point out the difficulties of propositions as such and of the church's articles and definitions of faith which "are propositions—simple or complex—and are not a priori free from the laws that govern propositions" (157).

It should be noted, secondly, that Küng regards his linguistic reflections simply as an "auxiliary argument" which ought not be given too great an importance (158). Actually Küng's reflections here are in no sense at all an argument against the possibility of *infallible* propositions because they are not even an argument against the possibility of *true* propositions. He explicitly states, after presenting his five propositions about propositions: "We do not mean that propositions are incapable of stating the truth, that all propositions are equally true and false, that they cannot correspond to the reality which they claim to express, that understanding is impossible" (161). All his argument really proves is "that propositions are by no means as clear as they seem to be, that they are rather fundamentally ambiguous and consequently can be understood differently by different people, that with the best intentions not all misunderstandings and misuse can be a priori excluded" (161). Who can quarrel with this conclusion? Apparently only those "scholastic" theologians who might object that "there are propositions—even propositions of faith—clear enough in themselves to exclude all misunderstandings, almost as clear in fact as $2 \times 2 = 4$" (161-162). One does not have to throw out the idea of infallibility in order to deal with such theologians.

The fact that Küng can state on one page, however, that "not . . . all propositions are equally true and false" (161) and on another that "propositions can be true *and* false" (170) suggests a certain unclarity, if not a strict logical contradiction, in Küng's thought. Lindbeck, like Rahner,[101] is among those who do not find Küng's clarification of his linguistic argument satisfactory. He therefore calls for a "much more careful analysis of the actual uses of dogmatic language than has heretofore been undertaken", an analysis that would be properly critical without getting entangled, as Küng seems to be, "in what look like sweeping attacks on the 'laws of thought' ".[102]

6. *The Real Problem: Papal Absolutism—Not Papal Infallibility:* The soundest and most valuable part of Küng's work on the papacy, both in *Structures* and in the present book, is his insight that "the basic problem . . . is still papal absolutism" (103). Vatican I, of course, explicitly stated that papal infallibility is "in no sense" absolute. And in both Vatican I and Vatican II one can find what Küng aptly calls "theoretical-abstract" restrictions on papal power. One might well argue that Vatican I sowed the seeds for making obsolete an absolutist papacy. But this does not alter the hard truth, pointed out by no one more clearly than Hans Küng, that neither Vatican I nor Vatican II produced any "realistic-practical" and juridical safeguards to protect the church against a pope

who abuses his ministry by absolutist, heretical or schismatic conduct. In fact, both councils closed their eyes to the very possibility of such conflict situations between pope and church which medieval Catholic theology and canon law took quite seriously (101-108).[103]

Juridical, constitutional safeguards against possible abuses of the papal office are not only compatible with the Catholic belief in papal primacy and infallibility; they are imperative for increasing the likelihood that the papacy be an instrument of supreme service and not of domination; they are imperative if there is ever to be an ecumenical papacy, a papacy for all Christians. These safeguards against papal absolutism will not take the form of that cumbersome conciliar machinery of the past, which caused almost as many problems as it solved. They will take the form of some of those tried means drawn from man's political experience, especially in the struggle against political absolutism. This does not mean that the Christ-intended Petrine ministry will be replaced by a parliament or a congress. But it means at least that the one who holds this ministry will be chosen by a much more representative segment of the church than has been the case for many centuries. And it also means that the holder of this important ministry will not be chosen for life, but for a fixed term of office so that the church has the option of dismissing him if he has not served the church well and of re-electing him if he has.

The only thing that Küng needs to be reminded of here is that papal absolutism and papal infallibility are not the same. To urge that tendencies toward papal absolutism be checked by the establishment of effective canonical safeguards is an unquestionably legitimate theological enterprise. To argue that papal absolutism cannot be checked without abandoning the dogma of papal infallibility is something that neither Küng nor anyone has yet proved.

Alternatives should and can be given to Küng's proposal which would truly lead to an ecumenically acceptable concept of papal infallibility, even if one of the first items in such alternative proposals might well be getting rid of the term "papal infallibility" altogether because of its manifestly misleading connotations. I have, in the course of my response to Küng, indicated several other elements that should be included in an alternative approach. Since this article is intended to be an evaluation of Küng's proposal, however, to begin to develop systematically such an alternative here would take us beyond the scope of this essay.

NOTES

1. *Strukturen der Kirche* (Freiburg: Herder 1962), pp. 342-343 (my trans.); cf. *Structures of the Church*, trans. S. Attanasio (New York: Nelson 1964), pp. 380-381.
2. While Charles Davis is correct in saying that he had already anticipated some of Küng's reinterpretation of infallibility in *A Question of Conscience* (New York: Harper and Row 1967), the main lines of it can be found not only in Karl Barth but in the reformers themselves. Cf. Davis, "Küng on Infallibility," *Commonweal* 93 (Feb. 5 1971) 445. Küng's position is actually much closer to that of Barth than to Calvin or Luther. Cf. *Structures*, pp. 352-366, 378-381, esp. 379, note 2. It is significant that Barth's negative attitude toward the very concept of infallibility represents, as will soon be evident, a departure from the Reformers.
3. Trans. Edward Quinn (Garden City, N.Y.: Doubleday 1971). See esp. pp. 175, 185, 193-199. Küng was already leaning toward the Calvin-Barth position in *The Church* (New York: Sheed and Ward 1967), pp. 341-342.
4. Proposals for rejecting the Vatican I dogma have already been made by recent Catholic authors. Since these authors did not have Küng's international reputation as a theologian their books did not create too much of a storm in the Catholic world. Cf. Bishop Francis Simons, *Infallibility and the Evidence* (Springfield, Ill.: Templegate 1968) and Francis Oakley, *Council Over Pope?* (New York: Herder and Herder 1969). When one reads Oakley's pointed critique (pp. 137-141) both of Küng's *Structures* and *The Church* it would almost seem as if Küng had revised his position accordingly in his new book. Those who heard Küng's lectures on infallibility in New York City a few years ago, however, already had an idea of the main lines of his present thesis.

has it, that "to the extent that" the church preserves the truth
of God it is "the pillar and mainstay of the truth". For Calvin
the church *is* the pillar and mainstay of the truth and the
truth of God *is* maintained in the church by the efforts of the
church and its ministry. Granted, nothing is said yet about
infallible councils or popes, but the solid foundation for a
dialogue on this other question is present in both Calvin and
Luther. Küng's starting point in *Infallible?* is something altogether different, as we shall see below, and the proposal
he offers for an ecumenical rapprochement actually leads him
away from the consensus of the Reformers, the Catholics and
the Orthodox that the church is, in some real sense, infallible
and that it can articulate or profess its faith infallibly.

35. My emphasis. Cf. Althaus, p. 7, note 15.
36. P. 462.
37. Althaus, p. 361.
38. *Ibid.*
39. I think, for example, of the fine essay by H. Fries, "Ex sese,
non ex consensu ecclesiae," in: *Volk Gottes—Festgabe für J.
Höfer*, ed. R. Bäumer and H. Dolch (Freiburg: Herder 1967)
which not only offers a sound and ecumenically helpful interpretation of this famous phrase from Vatican I, but also indicates how Karl Barth's critique of infallibility, which has
captivated Küng, has been significantly abandoned by Barth's
successor at Basel, Heinrich Ott. Cf. H. Ott, *Die Lehre des I.
Vatikanischen Konzils* (Basel 1963). Again, Küng does not
utilize the highly important essay of K. Rahner, "What is a
Dogmatic Statement," *Theological Investigations*, vol. V (Baltimore: Helicon 1966), originally presented to the Lutheran-
Catholic dialogue team in Germany. This essay provides part
of the basis of George Lindbeck's hope that even the Catholic dogma of papal infallibility might eventually "be so reduced in importance" that the separation of Christians would
no longer be justified. Cf. *The Future of Roman Catholic
Theology* (Philadelphia: Fortress 1970), pp. 110-111 and
117. Küng mentions, but does not incorporate into his thought,
Gustave Thils' *L'Infaillibilité Pontificale* (Gembloux 1969), a
study which makes it incorrect to conclude, as Küng does,
that the maximizing view of papal teaching authority held by
some of Pope Paul's advisors is the view that was defined by
Vatican I. From quite another perspective, even Charles Davis
recognizes that Küng's summary of the state of the question
of infallibility "is a slanted and not indisputable summary.
From a scholarly standpoint a more impartial weighing of the
pros and cons would be in order". *Commonweal* (Feb. 5
1971) 446. For this reason Davis concludes that the book is

"more an action in ecclesiastical politics than a contribution to theology".

40. Pp. 224-394.
41. Pp. 341-344, 444-480.
42. P. 343.
43. *Journal of Ecumenical Studies* I/1 (1964) 111. Lindbeck, *The Future of Roman Catholic Theology*, p. 105, cites the same passage as exemplifying the hopeful new developments in Catholic theology toward a reinterpretation of infallibility.
44. Recall, however, the concession Küng makes regarding conciliar infallibility that we mentioned above at note 15.
45. "An Ecumenical Boon?," *Commonweal* (Sept. 6 1968) 595.
46. Which is not necessarily the same thing as "mores" in the phrase "fides et mores" used at Trent and at Vatican I. Cf. J. David, "Glaube und Sitten: eine miβverständliche Formel," *Orientierung* 35/3 (Feb. 15 1971) 32-34 and the discussion in *Orientierung* 35/6 (March 31 1971) 70-72.
47. See my essay, "The Right of Catholics to Dissent from *Humanae Vitae*," *The Ecumenist* 8/1 (Nov.-Dec. 1969) 5-9.
48. It was Charles Davis, I believe, who, before his resignation from the Roman Catholic Church, distinguished between a "real" and a "fictitious" assent of bishops to papal teaching. In the latter case, surely verified on a wide scale after Vatican I because of that council's inability to dispatch its intended doctrine on the episcopate that would balance the definitions concerning the papacy, many bishops "accepted" and "assented to" the teaching of *Casti Connubii* primarily, if not solely, because it was papal teaching. How many of them actually gave a "real" assent to that teaching by thinking through and prayerfully reflecting upon the issue themselves? How many thought their episcopal task was primarily that of relaying or translating "the mind of Rome"? One can, with Küng (50), call such an attitude "unenlightened", but one must not lose sight of the fact that behind every unenlightened bishop there stands an unenlightened theologian who once taught the bishop-to-be about the responsibilities of bishops.
49. While it may be true that Küng can concede to Rahner (see note 54 below) that *Humanae Vitae* is not "infallible" without undermining his basic thesis, it also seems true that Küng never would have written this kind of book had he not started with the assumption that, according to the strict logic of Vatican I, *Humanae Vitae* was infallible. For then he would not have been able to set up his false dilemma: either accept *Humanae Vitae* fully or deny infallibility.
50. P. 369.
51. *StdZ* (Dez. 1970) 366-368; (März 1971) 153-155.

52. *StdZ* (März 1971) 154.—In a letter to Lady Simeon of Nov. 18, 1870 responding to her fears about Archbishop Manning's maximizing of the Vatican I dogma, Newman wrote: "Recollect men like the archbishop and Mr Ward said all the strong things they now say, before the Council. Such sayings did not trouble you then, why should they trouble you now? They certainly spoke without authority, before the Council was held; is it wonderful that (however little the Council has said) they should persevere now? Do not let such phantoms frighten you or make you sad." Quoted by C. S. Dessain, "Infallibility: What Newman Taught in Manning's Church," in: *Infallibility in the Church: An Anglican-Catholic Dialogue* (London: Darton, Longman and Todd 1968) p. 61.

53. *StdZ* (Dez. 1970) 368.

54. *StdZ* (Jan. 1971) 50-51. Nonetheless it is an important assumption he makes throughout the book, not just in the first chapter. Cf. pp. 67, 137, 174.

55. *StdZ* (Jan. 1971) 50-51.

56. Such an idea was explicitly proposed at Vatican I and was rejected. Cf. the proposed emendation number 45 and the response of Bishop Gasser, which indicates that the object of ecclesial/papal infallibility, as Vatican I intended to define it, extends only to those moral truths "which pertain in every respect to the deposit of faith"; such is not the case, he notes, for certain principles of the natural law. Cf. Mansi, 52, 1130 and 1224.—The bishops at Vatican I were also aware of the argument used by the minority group of Pope Paul's advisors on birth control—reported by Küng on p. 55—namely, that the popes had to have been guided by the Holy Spirit when they condemned something as morally evil, otherwise they would have been leading the whole church into error. But the Vatican I bishops were not persuaded by this argument to extend the object of infallibility to all moral questions. They thus were prepared to live with the possibility that popes could mislead the church when speaking on moral questions not intrinsically related to the deposit of faith. Since the bishops at Vatican I did not want to teach that the church was promised infallible guidance by the Holy Spirit on such moral questions several proposed emendations to the contrary were rejected. Cf. the handling of proposed emendations 56, 57 and 58 in Mansi 52, 1132-1134 and 1228.

57. I know personally of one archbishop, by no means an "old man", who seriously thinks that the Vatican I dogma means Pope Paul VI is "the greatest theologian in the world". Although one cannot ignore the disastrous pastoral consequences

that might result from such an archepiscopal attitude, one cannot help wondering about the quality of the theologian(s) who transmitted to this pastor such a magical concept of the papacy.

58. Pp. 249 and 310. For Küng's superb historical treatment of these conflict situations see pp. 249-341. More up to date and exceptionally valuable for distinguishing the Catholic from the unorthodox conciliar theories are the first four chapters of F. Oakley's, *Council Over Pope?*

59. This is not to say that the development of a systematic theology of the *fallibility* of the church, of councils and of the pope might not be the best context in which to discuss ecumenically the doctrine of infallibility.

60. Conciliar infallibility does not mean that councils cannot err or have not erred any more than papal infallibility means popes cannot or have not erred. For this reason Küng's citation of a contemporary Orthodox theologian to the effect that councils can err is not too helpful (p. 203). Martin Luther was by no means the first or the last Catholic to say popes and councils can and have erred. Cf. R. Bäumer, "Luthers Ansichten über die Irrtumsfähigkeit des Konzils und ihre theologiegeschichtlichen Grundlagen," in: *Wahrheit und Verkündigung: M. Schmaus zum 70. Geburtstag*, ed. L. Scheffczyk, W. Dettloff, R. Heinzmann (München 1967) 987-1003. Robert Bellarmine, *De romano pontifice* IV, 2, knows of only one Catholic theologian—Albert Pighius—who notes that the pope *cannot* publicly teach heresy!

61. Küng has studied Calvin on this point more than he has Luther. As was suggested in note 34, much more work has to be done on both of these great reformers before one judges that Küng's proposal truly leads to an ecumenical rapprochement with them and with the Christians standing in their traditions. It is clear that neither Luther nor Calvin, nor, I suspect, the majority of their spiritual heirs—not to mention the Orthodox—would be happy with Küng's treatment of "the truth of Scripture" (209-221) or with his assertion that neither church nor bible is infallible (218-219). As for the idea that God alone is infallible, Luther would argue that the apostles were "infallibles Doctores": proposition 59 of the Wittenberg Propositions of 1535 (WA 39/I, p. 48, lines 1 and 2). Proposition 61 states: ". . . It ought not be said of anyone: he cannot err in faith, except the universal church alone" (WA 39/I, 48, 3-6). This seems to rule out absolutely any notion of papal infallibility; but, as we indicated in note 60, Bellarmine could accept this proposition. We cite these words of Luther simply to emphasize again

that it is here, with the infallibility of the church, that a truly ecumenical dialogue on infallibility ought to begin.

62. Küng's own sketch of the Orthodox understanding of councils indicates that only certain Orthodox theologians would accept his solution (200-208); many would not, since it calls into question the infallibility of councils.

63. Cf. *StdZ* (Dez. 1970) 373-374 and (Jan. 1971) 58-59.

64. Pp. 366-368.

65. Pp. 366-375; 229-249.

66. Mansi 52, 1215.

67. Mansi 52, 1216-1217.

68. In view of the possibility, generally acknowledged by Catholic theologians, that popes can fall into heresy, it helps sharpen our understanding of the relationship of papal definitions to the faith of the church by pointing out that one reason the pope is bound to search out the faith of the church is that its faith is not necessarily the same as his faith.

69. Mansi 52, 1217.

70. *Journal of Ecumenical Studies* 5/4 (1968) 728.

71. Cf. Denzinger-Schönmetzer, *Enchiridion Symbolorum* . . . (Freiburg: Herder 1965) n. 3074 and note 46 above.

72. See esp. note 56.

73. *Constitution on the Church,* ch. III, n. 25, § 4. Küng cites this portion of the constitution on p. 73.

74. *Schema constitutionis de Ecclesia* (Vatican 1964), p. 97.

75. *Schema* (1964), p. 93. Cf. also the study by Fries mentioned in note 39 above.

76. *Schema* (1964), p. 98: ". . . sed consensum totius communitatis secum ferant et exprimant."

77. Contrast this with *Structures,* p. 371, where Küng says: "The necessity of a simultaneous or subsequent consensus of the episcopate is to be excluded, yet it is not to be maintained that the pope can define a truth without, as a basis, the *prior* existence of a consensus of the Church. . . . [The pope] may not define without the mind of the Church [sensus ecclesiae]." Küng also cites with approval the findings of R. Aubert to the same effect.

78. See note 24 above.

79. In addition to the conciliar documents we have already cited in this connection, a *votum* made by the Patriarch of Alexandria likewise serves to clarify the intention of Vatican I. The Patriarch wanted it to be made clear that, when defining, the pope does not add to the deposit of revelation nor does he act arbitrarily or alone, but must first (*prius*) seek out the doctrine of the universal church. The Patriarch was assured by Bishop Gasser, speaking for the deputation *de Fide,* that

his wish was in harmony with the sense of the definition. Mansi 52, 1127 and 1222.

80. See note 77.

81. Even an infallibly true definition, of course, is subject to all the historical limitations, incompleteness and sinfulness from which the pilgrim church is never completely free. Hence even an infallible definition can never be the absolutely last word the church can define on a matter of faith, nor can it ever be a perfect means of conveying the gospel to men. All this can and should be said without saying, however, that the definition is heretical or erroneous. On the distinction between error on the one hand and a dogma's inadequacy, incompleteness, "dangerousness" and its capacity to mislead on the other, cf. Rahner, *Theological Investigations* V, pp. 45-47; *StdZ* (Dez. 1970) 368-370; (März 1971) 155-156.

82. See the text from Augustine cited by Küng on p. 206, and Bellarmine, *De conciliis et ecclesia* II, 7, who says that the universal "praecepta morum" laid down by one council can be amended by another in the light of new *experience* and changes of time, place and persons. When these precepts are changed, Bellarmine explains, it is not because the matter was evil at the time the precept was made, but because the matter began to be evil when the circumstances changed.

83. *Institutes* IV, 8, 10: "They wish our faith to stand or fall according to their pleasure, that *whatever* they may have determined . . . may be implicitly received by our minds as *fully decided*, so that if they approve of *anything*, we must approve of the same *without any hesitation*. . . ." (my emphasis). Calvin makes it clear, however, in IV, 9, 8, that he does not wish to degrade the authority of councils. All he wants to establish is that Christians have the right to measure conciliar decisions against the Scriptures, something which, as can be seen below, contemporary Catholic theologians are also beginning to emphasize.

84. *StdZ* (Dez. 1971) 375.

85. This should not be understood as excluding the "norms" of historical-critical interpretation that must be applied to Scripture.

86. Rahner, *StdZ* (März 1971) 159.

87. *Ibid.*

88. Cf. Calvin, *Institutes* IV, 9, 8 and Küng, *Structures*, p. 348. Does Calvin's *praeiudicium* mean something more than Küng thinks when he translates it as "a provisional judgment"?

89. Cf. R. McCormick, "The Teaching Role of the Magisterium and of Theologians," *The Catholic Theological Society of*

America: Proceedings of the 24th Annual Convention (Yonkers, N.Y. 1970), esp. pp. 249-254.

90. Cf. Rahner, *StdZ* (Dez. 1970) 375 and the Vatican II *Decree on Ecumenism*, n. 11.

91. From the unpublished Report of the Conference dated March 18, 1971, p. 9.—It seems to me the only difference between this attitude and that of the Catholic who believes that a particular dogma is infallibly taught is that the Catholic is *sure* that this particular pronouncement not just "might", but *does* "contain" revealed truth.

92. *National Catholic Reporter* (March 26 1971) 12-A.

93. Space does not permit me here to deal with the question, immensely important for any full-scale study of infallibility: Have the Marian dogmas and even the Vatican I dogma of papal infallibility really met the conditions of infallibility? This question has to be raised anew, despite the almost universal assumption by Roman Catholics for more than a century that these are indeed infallible dogmas. In drawing up a systematic alternative to Küng's proposal, which cannot be done here, the precise question that would have to be treated is: Do these dogmas really express the faith of the *whole* Church, or only of the Roman Catholic Church? Catholic theologians might well answer this question differently today than they would have prior to the Second Vatican Council, especially in view of that council's teaching that the church of Jesus Christ subsists in, but is not co-extensive with the Roman Catholic Church. If a dogma can only be considered to be infallible when it "embodies the Church's unanimity", to use Tavard's phrase, then it is possible, in the light of what Vatican II considers the *whole* church to be, that these dogmas are not infallible, since they do not "express the consensus of the *whole* community", to use the language of the Vatican II *relatio* cited above in note 76. This does not mean the dogmas would not be *true*, but that they would not be *infallible*. But if they are not infallible, then, by definition, they *might* not be true. I personally see no sound reason for denying that these dogmas communicate certain aspects of the Christian message; I raise the question of their "binding force", to use a traditional but questionable formulation, simply in order to open up the possibility of new avenues that will permit freer ecumenical discussion of these controverted dogmas.

94. The Vatican II *Decree on the Bishops' Pastoral Office*, n. 13 sets the standard for episcopal teaching and preaching: "The bishops should present Christian doctrine in a manner adapted

to the needs of the times, that is to say, in a manner corresponding to the difficulties and problems by which people are most vexatiously burdened and troubled."

95. *StdZ* (Dez. 1970) 375; cf. Rahner's open letter to Cardinal Höffner of Cologne in *The Month* 231 (April 1971) 106 and his essay in *StdZ* (Juli 1970) mentioned in note 5.

96. *StdZ* (März 1971) 153.

97. *StdZ* (Dez. 1970) 376-377; (März 1971) 153, 159-160. Cf. also *Theological Investigations* V, p. 66.

98. *StdZ* (Dez. 1970) 377; (März 1971) 153.

99. Cf. *The Church*, p. 343 and *Structures*, pp. 389-394 where he even uses the same illustration of his point, namely, the ambiguity of the *sola fide* formulation, as he does in *Infallible?*, pp. 170-172.

100. *Commonweal* (Feb. 5 1971) 44.

101. *StdZ* (Dez. 1970) 368-370; (März) 155-156, 158-160.

102. "A Symposium on Infallibility: III—A Protestant Perspective," *America* (April 24, 1971) 432.

103. Cf. the references to *Structures* in note 58 above.

George
LINDBECK

It is now over a hundred years since the infallibility debate began, but the most recent phase of the discussion is taking a new turn. The central question is no longer that of truth, but of meaning. More and more the problem is whether dogmatic infallibility makes any sense, not whether it is true or false. This, to be sure, is scarcely surprising, for questions of meaning are urgent in our day. Most philosophical theologians, for example, are now preoccupied, not with the truth of talk about God, but with its meaningfulness. The crisis of teaching authority in the Church, whether of magisterium, Bible, or dogma, is a crisis of meaning. No one seems to be quite sure anymore of what anyone or anything means.

As far as infallibility is concerned, this shift in the character of the discussion has had its harbingers, but Hans Küng's recent book has made the change dramatically evident. As far as I am aware, he is the first well-known theologian, Catholic or non-Catholic, to suggest explicitly that the concept of dogmatic infallibility is meaningless. This revolutionizes the terms of the argument, and the Church authorities will be well advised to refrain from hasty judgment. Is it really heretical to say, not that a dogma is false, but that it doesn't make sense? Even if the Holy Spirit preserves the Church's most solemn pronouncements from falsehood, does this necessarily imply that they can't be or become nonsensical?

From a Protestant perspective, it would be convenient to

be able to agree with Küng, but this is unfortunately difficult because of the way in which he attacks the meaningfulness of "infallible" or "guaranteed" propositions. This is one of the points with which we shall deal in what follows. After commenting on the present crisis of meaning, I shall argue that probably every religion, and certainly Christianity, is committed to affirming the infallibility of at least some of its central affirmations.

The relation of this infallible core to the official, and in part changing, doctrinal formulations of the Churches is the topic of a second section. Only in the third part shall we finally find ourselves in a position to discuss what is involved in claiming, not only that there are infallible dogmas, but an infallible teaching office such as was defined by Vatican I.

The approach throughout is functional, contextual and linguistic; that is, I have tried to focus on the ways in which affirmations of faith and official dogmas actually operate within the context of religious language systems and forms of life. Nevertheless, my own thinking has also been influenced by the rather more metaphysical treatments of these problems represented especially by Karl Rahner and Bernard Lonergan, but this has happened in ways which they might not recognize nor approve, and for which they certainly cannot be held responsible. Their helpfulness—if I may be allowed to underline the obvious—is in understanding what dogmatic and magisterial infallibility might mean, not in accepting the Roman Catholic version of these doctrines, for understanding is an act quite distinct from acceptance. Indeed, it is the presupposition quite as much for denying an affirmation as for affirming it.

Nevertheless, the sense which it seems to me finally possible to find infallibility is in many ways very different from what has been traditionally supposed, and this makes it necessary to re-evaluate the doctrine from the ecumenical and Reformation perspectives which are my own. This re-evaluation concludes the third and final section of the essay.

I. The Need for Infallible Propositions

Reflection on what statements mean is, of course, as old as

the theological enterprise. What is new in our day is that the problems have greatly multiplied. In part this is because in every transitional period such as ours, concepts and values become problematic. In addition there are special difficulties that arise from the increased awareness of the contextual character of meaning, on the one hand, and of human historicity on the other. We need to remind ourselves of these three general factors before plunging into the debate about how to deal with them.

First, then, the Church's authority, not to mention infallibility, is being shaken by the massive and rapid transmutation of both the infra-structures and the superstructures of our society. Both the sociological base and the theoretical constructs are being revolutionized. The West is being progressively de-Christianized, and the Constantinian establishment of religion which has prevailed for fifteen hundred years is now everywhere vanishing. The forms in which teaching authority was institutionalized and the corresponding attitudes still persist, even though they are becoming increasingly ineffective. Further, old theories, whether ideological or theological, have less and less application to what is actually happening, and new ones either have not been formulated or have not been accepted. Part of the problem here is simply that the changes have been so sudden that responsible reformulation and reinterpretation haven't had a chance to catch up. In this respect our age probably resembles the first generations when Christianity moved from a Jewish to a Hellenistic environment more than it does any intervening period. Then as now there was incredible confusion about the fundamental import of the gospel. Gnostic as well as other heresies threatened to swamp what we consider the Christian mainstream. It took centuries for the meaning of the faith to be coherently and comprehensively restated in Greek terms, and the end product of the process was in some respects immensely different from the original. Without being specifically denied, its Jewishness had largely vanished. Perhaps something similar will happen to the Roman doctrine of infallibility. Maybe it will simply become irrelevant, though never repealed.

A second consideration is that we are now much more keenly aware than in the past of the situational or contextual character of all meaning. The linguistic analysts, especially Wittgenstein, speak sometimes of meaning as a function of "forms of life". Unless we know the ways language operates in the detailed behavior of individuals and communities, we do not know its signification. Words and concepts have meanings insofar as they have uses, and to know their meaning is, at least on one level, to know their use. This is why knowledge of the situation or context is of vital importance, for it is the context which both occasions and explains the When, the Why and the How—that is, the meaning—of what we say. At least part of the question regarding the meaning of infallibility, therefore, concerns the functions or uses it can or should have in the life of the Church.

Also contributing to the problem of meaning is the immense growth of historical knowledge. This is the point of which Küng is especially aware. We have become much more conscious of historical relativity and of intellectual and cultural pluralism. What a given form of words means in one epoch, society or intellectual discipline is often very different from what it means in another; or conversely, what look like entirely dissimilar affirmations may function similarly, may have the same meaning, in different settings. Sometimes what was said in another period or culture may be basically inexpressible in ours simply because an appropriate language or conceptuality is not available; and such difficulties cannot always be solved by partial borrowing from the ancient or the foreign source because what would have to be borrowed is a total world view or even a whole form of life. It is not *a priori* impossible that such difficulties are now assailing the dogma of infallibility, rendering it meaningless, not only in the practical sense of irrelevant, but in the strong sense of unintelligible.

This basically is what Küng affirms. The neuralgic point, the first premise, of his case against magisterial infallibility appears to be that it is nonsense to talk of infallible propositions. Because of the historical and cultural relativity of all human languages and conceptualities, a proposition "can be true *and* false".[1] This is obviously an important statement from his point of view, for he carefully underlines the "and". Propositions are thus intrinsically susceptible to error, and like all other human statements, a dogmatic proposition also is not infallible, invulnerable to falsity, but is rather fallible. It may be permanently true, but it cannot be guaranteed against error. One cannot be sure it will remain true.

Now this move of Küng provides him an expeditious way of winning his case. It annihilates the foundations of the magisterial infallibility to which he objects. If the Church through its teaching office is incapable of producing infallible propositions simply because there are no such things, then the infallibility of the Church must be reduced—or exalted—to God's wondrous promise that "it will persist in the truth *in spite* of all ever possible errors",[2] and, in order to avoid misunderstanding, such an infallibility is better called "indefectibility" or "perpetuity".[3]

The conclusion is admirable. A Protestant speaking from the Reformation perspective need not say less, nor need a Catholic say more. When properly developed, it could provide, I believe, all that is necessary in this area in order to safeguard both the authority of the Gospel and Christian freedom, both unity and diversity in the Church. This point we shall have occasion to deal with later in our discussion. At the moment it is necessary only to emphasize that my quarrel is *not* with Küng's contention that "magisterial infallibility" can and should be supplanted by "ecclesial indefectibility".

It is his first premise which troubles me, and for much the same reasons that it has troubled many Catholics. The German bishops concentrate on this in their statement on Küng's book,[4] and it is also the problem which chiefly disturbs Rahner amid all his other questions about Küng's procedure.[5] Is it really the case that all true propositions can become infected with error, with falsehood? Above all, does this hold for all religious statements, for all affirmations of Christian faith, for all—not just some—dogmas? Is it true, for example, of "Jesus is Lord"?

Now Küng does not want to raise doubts about the truth, the abiding and unshakable truth, of this or any other of the fundamental credal affirmations. He is emphatically within the mainstream of the historic Christian tradition and, at least to Protestant eyes, is definitely a Roman Catholic also. Why then does he systematically use language which suggests such doubts? He never cites the fundamental articles as examples of fallible propositions, but neither does he exempt them from his sweeping generalizations.[6]

The only explanation which I can think of is that he has objections—which, however, he never articulates in this book—against the ancient and familiar distinction between judgments or affirmations, on the one hand, and the forms of words or sets of concepts which are employed to articulate them, on the other. According to this, the act of judging is either true or false, with no mean in between, but this does not hold of the verbal or conceptual vehicle in which it is expressed. It is, however, as if Küng had never heard of what St. Thomas calls the "second act of the intellect". It is as if he had never heard of what in contemporary English-language discussions is generally called the distinction between "propositions" or "statements" and "sentences". Yet it is hard to suppose that he does not know about such devices and the associated two-valued logics, laws of thought (identity, contradiction and excluded middle) and "correspondence" theories of truth. It is difficult to imagine that he has not often been exposed to the suggestion that the same basic affirmation, such as "Jesus is Lord", may be expressed in different languages or conceptualities (e.g., "Jesus is Messiah", "God-man", etc.), some more and some less adequate, but that *qua* affirmation, it always remains either true or false. Conversely, the same sentence—let us once again cite "Jesus is Lord"—may be used to express different propositions, not only true ones, but false ones such as "Jesus is the one for whose sake it is mandatory to kill heretics". But that doesn't make the same proposition true *and* false. It simply means that the same sentence can be used to enunciate different propositions. In this approach, every true proposition, including those about the impermanent, are eternally true, incapable of being erroneous, and in this improper sense, "infallible". To use a Scholastic example, in the proposition, "Socrates is now sitting", the "now" refers to a specific moment in Socrates' life, and so if there was ever a time at which it was true, it is always and infallibly true. This way of avoiding the contradictory attribution of both truth and falsity to the same statement is no doubt familiar to Küng. There must be something about it which he finds unsatisfactory. What it is I do not know, and there is no point in speculating, for he gives us little evidence on which to build.

In any case, however, it would seem best not to try to dispose of doctrinal infallibility by ignoring distinctions between a proposition and a sentence or between an affirmation and the concepts used in making it. These have survived in one form or another since Aristotle, and their eclipse under the impact of Hegelianism and German idealism proved temporary, at least among English-speaking professional logicians and philosophers. Religious thinkers, perhaps especially Catholics rebelling against too much of the wrong kind of Scholastic logic, seem more inclined at the moment than their secular colleagues to propose complicated and puzzling theories of truth which are far removed from traditional ones. Thus they get into the odd position of attacking the presumed irrationality of dogmatic infallibility by means of theories of propositional truth which are positively anti-rational to most secular specialists in these problems. To put a polemical edge on the matter, what Thomas Aquinas has to say about the logical properties of propositions is much more interesting to non-Catholics than are Küng's or Leslie Dewart's theories.

After saying all this, however, it must be admitted that Küng would probably not be very much impressed by this argument that his case against the possibility of infallible dogmas is philosophically suspect. At least in this book, he does not pretend to be a philosopher. His fundamental objections to dogmatic and magisterial infallibility are undoubtedly theological, and the sympathetic reader will be inclined to say that it is only because he has presented his case poorly that he has made it appear to rest on a debatable theory of propositions. He is, after all, in a sense a disciple of Karl Barth, and that makes it unlikely that he is to be included in the apparently growing group of Catholic as well as Protestant theologians who seem to think that points of faith can be decided by non-theological considerations. He probably agrees that neither philosophy, logic, science or history, nor appeals to the contemporary experience of the relativity of all meaning and truth, can be the court of final appeal. The question of the possibility of infallible dogmas is religious and must ultimately be settled for the Christian on specifically Christian grounds.

But how is this to be done? What is the proper procedure in debating theological questions in a properly theological way? What, to use traditional formulations, is the right relation between philosophy and theology, reason and faith? How can we allow for the modern awareness of the contextuality and historicity of meaning and truth and yet not permit this to control what we as Christians believe? These are the questions which are debated these days under the forbidding name of "methodology". Usually it is not necessary to articulate what we think on such knotty matters in order to get on with our discussions, but unfortunately this seems to be impossible when trying to think about the issues raised by the current debate over infallibility and teaching authority. We have said that this debate centers on the question of meaning, but it could perhaps be even better identified as a controversy over proper theological methodology. In any case, it is necessary to say something about the methodological problem of the relation of theology to non-theological considerations. This will serve as an introduction to the discussion of the specifically religious problem of infallibility.

Very briefly, then, the approach which we shall use is one which attempts to settle religious issues on religious grounds. With the exception of extreme Protestant liberals and Catholic modernists, all theologians have assented to this in theory, though by no means always in practice—indeed, one of the major complaints of the Protestant Reformers against late medieval Scholasticism was that it substituted reason for faith, Aristotle for the Gospel. This initial dictum, then, is ambiguous, but it can perhaps be sufficiently clarified for our purposes by referring back to the problem of propositional truth. If religious issues are to be settled on religious grounds, then no non-theological theory of propositions can be used to decide the question of whether dogmatic infallibility is either meaningful or possible. That question is independent of what one believes is the correct analysis of propositions in non-religious domains. Religious discourse has its own integrity, and no matter what is the best way to analyze propositions in other realms and for other purposes—whether in terms of two-valued logics, or in terms of Küng's view that they can be both true *and* false—this does not determine the appropriate way to talk about the central affirmations of the Christian faith.

This does not imply, however, that we can or should avoid the use of philosophical notions in theological discussions. Insofar as both enterprises are looked at as involving disciplined reflection of a certain kind on the uses of language, the distinction between them is somewhat arbitrary. Philosophy, from this perspective, is defined as the analysis of the non-religious uses of language, and theology as the analysis of its religious uses. But as it is ordinary human words which we employ in speaking about God, so it is often helpful to know how these words function outside the religious domain (i.e., "philosophically") in order to understand their religious (i.e., "theological") uses. Philosophical analysis of the first set of usages is often highly enlightening for the second, and mistakes arise only when the first is made to legislate for the second; that is, when philosophical considerations are made normative for theology.

Thus the examination of the religious meaning of infallibility to which we shall now turn employs philosophical notions just as freely as does either traditional or modern Roman Catholic theology whether this be of the "scholastic", or "transcendental", or some other variety. Its philosophical tools, however, are more those of linguistic analysis than of Aristotelian Thomism or phenomenological existentialism. This does not involve a programmatic commitment to a particular philosophical school. It is simply that I find some of the concepts and techniques developed by the analysts helpful in clarifying the issues involved in dogmatic and magisterial infallibility. I shall therefore use these in what are perhaps sometimes rather irregular—but I hope not inconsistent—ways, and I shall supplement them by borrowings from other philosophies when these seem theologically illuminating. Thus a kind of Thomistic distinction, which we have already reviewed, between a proposition and a sentence, or more precisely, between an affirmation and its verbal or conceptual vehicle, helps us, I believe, to make a religiously crucial point—one which Küng obscures. This procedure runs the risk of eclectic incoherence, of double-truth theories, of becoming trapped in a morass of mutually inconsistent philosophies, but if this danger is avoided, it is the only way of maintaining the integrity of the theological task.

It is not only to Protestants such as Karl Barth that one could appeal for a defense of this view of the relation of philosophy and theology, but also to Catholics—most notably Thomas Aquinas himself. Recent historical work has made us well aware that, contrary to a certain traditional caricature, he did not adopt Aristotelian philosophy *en bloc* and then build his theology on top of it. He borrowed freely from many sources: from Aristotle came the technical concepts of form and matter, and of act and potency; from Platonists, notions of participation; and from Avicenna, the distinction between essence and existence. The test was not whether these ideas were correct in their original non-Christian settings, but whether they could be effectively adapted to the theological task of understanding the faith.

It is in the same spirit that we shall utilize such concepts as that of a "religious language system" or a "form of life". They will be used as non-technically and informally as possible, so that their meaning can be construed from their context, not by reference back to other writers. The purpose is not definitively to adjudicate the problem of infallibility—such questions never are neatly settled once for all—but to see whether new light can be thrown on it by conceptualizing it in a somewhat different way than usual. This can be discovered only by trying, and so what follows should be regarded as an experiment.

What then should be said about infallible propositions from a religious perspective? It would seem that the case against them collapses. There are the strongest possible religious reasons for insisting, not only on the possibility, but on the actuality, of infallible affirmations. This, as we shall see, does not necessarily mean that the Roman Catholic or any other magisterium is infallible. What we are talking about is the inevitability of infallibility, not only for Catholicism, but for Protestantism, not only for Christianity, but also for non-Christian religions.

The infallibility which we have in mind is stronger than "incapable of being false". We have already seen that within two-valued logics this is a property of all true propositions. In addition to being permanently true, an infallible proposition has that characteristic of being "guaranteed" to which Hans Küng—perhaps mistakenly—thinks he objects.

That which guarantees it, however, is not necessarily any particular teaching authority, but the whole religion, the whole language system, the whole form of life of which it is a part. The relationship can equally well be stated in reverse order: those affirmations which guarantee, which ground, a religion are for it infallible. These are those central propositions which are essential to its identity and without which it would not be itself. They are sure, certain and unquestionable, because to suppose that it is possible that they might ever be shown to be false is to envision the disappearance of this particular religion, of the faith by which one lives. The believer can, of course, envision this possibility, either abstractly or by having real doubts, but insofar as he is within the circle of faith, the central credal affirmations are essential, unquestionable, infallible.

There is nothing subjective about the property of infallibility when it is looked at in this way. It is not dependent on the psychological or existential certainty of the believer, or on the degree of his trust, confidence or faith. One can agree that "Jesus is the Son of God" is an infallible proposition within the Christian language system even if one thinks of this as a piece of baseless mythology. Further, the property of infallibility is independent of whether anyone is reflectively conscious of this fact. The adherents of primitive religions are unaware that some of their beliefs are infallible and others are not. On the level of popular piety, Roman Catholics, not to mention other Christians, are sometimes in a similar situation. They do not, for example, discriminate between the logical status of "Catholics should go to Mass on Sunday" and "Catholics should believe that Jesus is the Son of God". But an outside observer would quickly discover, even if no one actually informed him, that one of these statements is not essential and the other is essential and infallible within the Catholic language system. In short, and stated abstractly, infallibility may be regarded as the objective property of unquestionability derived from the logically indispensable role which an affirmation plays within a given religion.

This is not only an objectivist view of infallibility, but also a contextualist one, and therefore the character of the infallibility attributed to a given statement varies depending on its location or role within the language to which it belongs. In religious discourse, the infallibility connected with the central affirmations of faith is primary, while that which arises from the syntax of the language is secondary. This is not the same as the distinction which a Scholastic might make between the infallibility of the first premises, the chief articles, of faith and their necessary deductive consequences or implications. In a deductive system, the conclusions have exactly the same certainty, the same infallibility, as the premises, no more and no less. Thus, both the chief articles of faith and their necessary implications have what might be called "primary infallibility", even though the latter are derived from the former.

What we are calling secondary or syntactical infallibility is of a rather different kind, for it is not directly derived from the central affirmations, but rather from the "depth grammar" or the fundamental logical syntax of a language. A distinctive way of construing reality, a kind of picture of the world, is embedded in the most general structures of a language. The Hopi Indian tongue, for example, is said to be able to express certain space-time relations of which English is incapable and, conversely, it excludes other relations which to us are commonplace.[7] Even if this is a poor illustration, still it makes the point that unquestioned, and in this sense infallible, metaphysical commitments are involved in every language.

This depth grammar both resembles and differs from the more familiar notions of "basic presuppositions" or "necessary transcendental conditions" (Rahner). On the one hand, both fundamental syntactical structures and fundamental presuppositions are in an indirect sense unquestioningly and thus infallibly affirmed by their users even though they are usually not aware that they are doing this; but, on the other hand, it is wrong from the linguistic point of view to speak of this substratum as somehow the basis for the certainty of the central affirmations of a religion, and this is contrary to what those who speak of "presuppositions" or "necessary conditions" generally do. It is better to think of this syntactical infallibility as secondary, for syntax is necessary only in the sense that it enables the speakers of a given language to say what they intend or want to say. If they do not want to affirm the central infallibilities of a religion, they are free to abandon the syntactical ones. That is, they can stop speaking the language, they can change religions. This is admittedly often difficult to do in practice—that is why individuals as well as whole societies often remain implicit adherents of a given religion, continuing to use its syntax, even after they have ceased to believe explicitly—but still it does happen, even if slowly.

Another important distinction between types of infallibility arises from the different ways in which religions regard or refer to themselves. One might say that some attribute more universal or higher levels of infallibility to themselves, and therefore also to their fundamental assertions, then do others. Primitive religions, for example, typically exclude all foreigners and strangers from the local or tribal cult and thus, in effect, claim no more than that they are true, are infallible, only for the in-group, not for those outside. In partial contrast, the mystery cults of the early centuries, as well as many contemporary religious movements, are open to whoever is interested, but still do not consider themselves the best or right religion for everyone. Some religions—certain forms of Buddhism might be examples—view themselves as universally the highest and best within space, but not necessarily within time. Perhaps new avatars will come who will surpass or replace the old. Only monotheistic historical religions such as Judaism, Christianity, and Islam have a higher, more universal viewpoint which enables them to make the self-referential claim that they are infallible, guaranteed to the end of time. Without a God who rules the universe and all of history, and who has in some sense definitively revealed himself, a religion does not have the language or conceptuality to affirm that it will never be surpassed.

Of all religions, however, Christianity is the most absolutely—or outrageously—infallibilist, and therefore the one least capable of surrendering the notion of infallible dogmas. It alone affirms that the God who is ultimate reality and truth has fully and definitively communicated himself for us men and our salvation in an historically locatable and empirically tangible person, Jesus. There are three infallibilities here, each more absolute than any which most other religions maintain. First, there is the assertion that it is the ultimate and unconditioned reality, the God above all gods, with whom we have to do in Jesus Christ. Most religions are content to traffic with lesser deities. Second, it is said that God's self-communication is final and unsurpassable, as full and complete as it can be under the conditions of human existence. Other religions have notions of incarnation, but only Christianity says that there is only a single unsurpassable instance of it. Others also talk about revelation but, with the possible exception of Islam, only Christianity claims that this is now closed and completed, that the publicly authoritative variety will not be added to until the coming of the Messiah, Jesus, at the end of history. Finally, there is the absolute particularity which Christianity ascribes to the full presence of the ultimate in space and time. This presence was unsurpassably objectified in a specific East Mediterranean country some two millennia ago in a man about whom a good many empirically detailed stories are told.

These three infallibilities are, to be sure, a unified affirmation, the affirmation that the full self-communication of the Ultimate Mystery under the conditions of human space and time is the man, Jesus Christ. This is the central dogma, the Christological core, of the faith, and it is infallible in the double sense of both being guaranteed by and guaranteeing the entirety of Christian language and life.

What is usually thought of as the problem of dogmatic infallibility does not arise here, but rather in reference to other affirmations which must be made in order to speak authentically and effectively about the Christological core and its manifold implications for all of life. Although their infallibility is derivative, it is also genuine, because they also are essential and therefore guaranteed parts of the language system which is necessary if Christians are to speak as they should. It is to a consideration of the character of their infallibility that we must now turn.

II. The Problem of Dogmatic Infallibility

When dogmas are thought of as what must necessarily, and therefore infallibly, be said in order to speak a religious language well, it is evident that a distinction should be drawn between what is necessary for individuals or for particular groups and what is necessary for the whole community. Normally only the latter are called "dogmas", and to this usage we shall conform. We must also distinguish between dogmatic affirmations on the level of ordinary religious language and their reflex articulation on the secondary level of informal or formal theological thought. The first level is fundamental, for no affirmation is really essential to a religion unless it is needed for proper worship, preaching, exhortation and action. The secondary level of theological discourse consists of talk about the primary uses of the language and attempts to distinguish between the essential and non-essential, the dogmatic and the non-dogmatic, aspects. In this perspective, theological doctrines are second-order statements about what is necessary on the primary level. These statements may be mistaken about what is in fact essential, they are not guaranteed by the total language system in its primary uses, and consequently there is no certainty that what they assert as infallible is infallible. Nevertheless, in almost all the so-called higher religions, some of these theological formulations acquire the status of official or quasi-official dogmas, creeds or confessions, and this expresses the conviction of the community of believers that these statements do in fact articulate infallible first-order dogmas. If it is further claimed that the teaching authority cannot err in its judgment on these matters, then we have a doctrine of magisterial infallibility and, by extension, of the infallibility of officially defined dogmas, such as was enunciated at

Vatican I. This is the heart of the present controversy, but before we turn to it, we must try to get clear on the nature of the infallibility or necessity which belongs to dogmas before they are defined, and which their definition does not create, but simply recognizes.

The problem here is that of the "mutability of infallibility". All the problems of dogmatic, as distinct from magisterial, infallibility are summed up in this phrase. It applies, however, only to what we have called derivative dogmas. The central affirmations are those which are essential to self-identity, and so their infallibility is as permanent as the religion itself. But derivative dogmas can apparently gain, and perhaps also lose, infallibility. Not everything which is at one time necessary to the adequate functioning of a religion and its language is always necessary.

This, of course, is an odd concept. It is not customary to speak of infallibility as a changeable property of affirmations. On the contrary, immutability and infallibility are often identified, and so what is immutably true is treated as infallibly true, and *vice versa*. But the disadvantage of this usage, as we have already observed, is that it leads to confusion, because it then becomes impossible within two-valued logics to distinguish between an infallible statement and any true affirmation whatsoever. Within such systems of logic, all truths are immutably true, but that doesn't make them infallible. Further, it seems to be difficult to do justice to the permanently indispensable role of the central affirmations if one abandons the notion of immutable truth. Consequently it seems best—not only for "secular" logical reasons but for specifically religious ones—totally to divorce the idea of "infallible" from "immutable" and to identify it simply with "guaranteed".

This problem of the mutability of infallibility is built into the structure of Christian faith to a greater degree than in the case of any other religion. There is a peculiar combination of definiteness and flexibility in the implications of its central affirmations. These affirmations focus, as we have seen, on empirically identifiable particularities, and are therefore definite, but the particularities are not those of a legal code, or cultic practices, or even of a book, but are rather those of the story of a people and, most especially, of a single man.

The definiteness becomes evident when one contrasts Christianity with non-historical religions in which the supremely divine is seen as a widely diffused quality of men or things. Here the fundamental assertions are universal statements about universals, and thus, by the very nature of the case, have a certain vagueness and indefiniteness which makes it possible to interpret and apply them without self-contradiction in an almost infinite variety of even mutually incompatible ways. As long as one stays within certain limits, one can consistently turn them into abstract philosophies or poetries of things in general. Both Hinduism and Buddhism provide good examples of these various processes. The same things happen within Christianity, of course, but only at the cost of doing violence to the logic of the faith. This helps explain why it is especially in Christianity that mutual anathematizing has occurred and why, at the worst, religious wars have been fought over points of dogmatic definition. The trouble arises from Christian definiteness. The Christian language does not simply contain the statement, "God is love" or "Love is God", but proceeds to define love in what are at once both highly complex and very precise ways by telling a story which spans the universe from beginning to end and climaxes in a particular life, death, and resurrection.

On the other hand, however, the fact that the particularity of the Christian affirmations centers on a person, a life, gives them a flexibility which is lacking when infallibility is concentrated, as in Judaism and Islam, in law or a book, in the Torah or Koran. The absoluteness of a specific code is best maintained simply by obeying, not modifying it, while that of a book is preserved by simply repeating it. Christians have also often done both these things with their laws and their book, but they have a higher authority to which they can appeal against such rigidities. Their final norm is a Person and a Life which, while it often has quite precise implications for how they should believe and behave, must be applied anew from situation to situation. Thus the specifically Christian problem of infallibility is not only that its central affirmations are infallible from every angle, from a universal viewpoint, and not only that they focus on particularities, but that these particularities are of such a kind that they have varying though definite consequences for how believers should act or think. The question, "Is this an essential Christian affirmation?" must often be answered with either a "yes" or a "no"—not both—and yet these answers do not always remain the same. In other words, one and the same affirmation may at one time be infallible and at other times fallible; an infallible, a guaranteed, dogma is not necessarily immutably such.

Protestants and Catholics have historically tried to handle this infallibility of the mutable, or mutability of the infallible, in different ways. Protestants have tried to solve the problem by denying the infallibility of post-biblical developments, while Catholics have minimized their mutability, but it would seem that neither can be surrendered without doing violence to the logic of the faith. The unchangeable faith must be proclaimed afresh in changing circumstances. God spoke his final Word in Jesus Christ, but he still speaks new words which are authoritative and binding, not only for individuals, but for the Christian community. Even Protestants recognize this in practice, though their theology generally lacks the concepts to do justice to it. The Reformers accepted the non-scriptural language of the ancient creeds. They formulated confessions of their own which we now see made as new affirmations not found explicitly in the Bible to a considerably greater degree than they realized. In recent times, the Barmen Declaration against the German Christians who compromised with the Nazis has dogmatic force for many Protestants, while the condemnation of slavery and even of segregation, even though these are not found in the Bible, are treated in practice as infallible dogmas—and rightly so!—by many people who abhor the very sound of the words.

Just as Protestants have failed to find categories for adequately conceptualizing the binding, guaranteed or infallible element in dogma, so Catholics have not succeeded in doing justice to its mutability. Up until one hundred fifty years ago, everyone, Catholics and Protestants alike, thought basically in terms of immutability; and this involved both groups in impossible intellectual gymnastics. Catholics postulated two-source theories of revelation according to which all doctrine not found explicitly in the Bible had been handed down orally from generation to generation, while Protestants either argued that their doctrines were simply the reproduction in brief form of what a purportedly infallible Bible says, or else tried to ignore two thousand years of history, of tradition, and held, in the famous phrase, that "the Bible and the Bible alone is the religion of Protestants".

The accumulating weight of historical evidence, however, has gradually made the old notions of immutability untenable. Protestants learned to think of the Bible as an historical book and, beginning especially with Newman, Catholics have come to view dogma as historical, as developing. This broke the old connection between immutability and infallibility. Infallibility was seen as a property which a truth need not always have, but which could be gained in the course of time. This, however, was only a partial concession to mutability, for according to the standard theories of development, once a doctrine has acquired infallibility, it can never again lose it. The process is irreversible. Truths of faith may not be permanently infallible in the sense of always having been explicitly known, affirmed and guaranteed since the earliest days of the Church, but once they are guaranteed, their infallibility is irrevocable.

It is this notion of the irreversibility of infallibility which seems to be the greatest source of difficulty in contemporary Roman Catholic discussions. According to the critics, it does not take sufficient account of change and thus supports dangerous rigidities. And yet there are grave difficulties in suggesting that a doctrine may not only gain, but also lose infallibility. It seems, among other things, to contradict what Vatican I says about the irreformability of dogmatic definitions. It suggests that the Marian, papal and sacramental dogmas of the past can lose their infallibility, can cease to be binding. And if this could happen to some dogmas, why couldn't it happen to all? Isn't the door opened to complete historical relativism, so that it becomes impossible to say that any affirmations, not even "Jesus is Lord", are permanent, irrevocable, unchangeable parts of Christian belief?

These objections sum up, in effect, the contemporary Roman Catholic problem of dogmatic infallibility, so we must now see whether they can be met by the contextual-linguistic approach we are employing.

First, there can be no question of total capitulation to relativism. By the very nature of the case, as we have seen, infallibility is an essential, not accidental or changeable, property of those central affirmations of a religion which define what the religion is. However it might be expressed, whether in the Greek conceptuality of "Jesus is Lord" or in the Hebrew conceptuality of "Jesus is the Messiah", or in some other way perhaps yet undreamt of, the underlying judgment that Jesus is unsurpassably important for all dimensions of the universe in which human beings live is unchangeably essential, unchangeably infallible, within the language system of the New Testament writers as well as the language systems of most of the people who have called themselves Christian since. Conjoined with this, there are innumerable other affirmations which are also unchangeably infallible simply because under all possible historical circumstances they are essential to the meaning of the central dogmas—without them they would not be the same affirmation. "God is love" and "Thou shalt love thy neighbor as thyself" will suffice as examples.

Most of these propositions have never been officially defined by any Church. As in the case of the examples we just cited, this is in part because they are so obviously necessary to the integrity of Christian speech, action and faith that dogmatization would be superfluous. But there is also another reason at work. The fundamental way in which we come to know the essential, the infallible, truths of the faith, whether these be changeable or unchangeable, is by learning how to use ordinary Christian language correctly and effectively in prayer, praise, admonition and preaching. This is the fundamental, primary knowledge of the faith. It constitutes that *sensus fidelium* of which the theologians speak. It is more like a skill than it is like explicit, reflective theological learning. To use the kind of example of which some linguistic analysts are fond, it is more like knowing how to play tennis well than it is like being able to analyze verbally the essential elements in a good tennis stroke. Or, to cite a more traditional analogy, it is more like that "knowledge by connaturality" of which St. Thomas speaks, whereby the virtuous person knows intuitively what is virtuous behavior, rather than like theoretical, verbalizable knowledge of virtue. Thus instead of relativistically dissolving the unconditionally necessary elements in Christian discourse, the approach we are exploring suggests that they are much more extensive and pervasive than even in traditional views. As in the case of natural languages—though, admittedly, with differences which we need not go into here—the man who speaks a given religious language well knows and affirms as necessary, and even unchangeably necessary, far more things on the level of use than he will ever be able reflexively to grasp.

Yet this emphatic denial of total relativism still leaves us with part of our problem. Christians not only worship and preach, they also reflect on these primary uses of their language. They do theology in formal and informal ways. They become not only speakers of the Christian tongue, they also become grammarians and linguists who try to distinguish reflectively between the essential and accidental, the infallible and fallible parts of their discourse. Sometimes they even find it desirable or necessary, usually because of controversies which they believe threaten serious damage to the language of faith, to formulate dogmas, creeds and confessions. They officially designate certain of their beliefs as crucially important for the great mass of implicitly held yet necessary and guaranteed convictions.

We see, then, that theological statements in general and official doctrines in particular are not the main instruments for the communication of Christian truth, because that happens chiefly through the vastly richer and fuller concrete language of scriptural stories, liturgy, devotion and proclamation. This is the primary religious language, not only emotively and volitionally but also propositionally. It is an intellectualistic error to suppose that the brief and abstract formulations of official doctrine can do more than express a very small part of the truth to which the intellect assents in the act of faith. Unless they are embedded in the living matrix of Christian language in its primary uses, they are quite literally unintelligible. St. Thomas himself makes a similar point when he suggests that the God-talk of pagan philosophers is from a Christian perspective meaningless: "Un-believers . . . do not believe that God exists under the conditions that faith determines; and hence they do not truly believe in a God." [8] Or one may think of scientific theories which can be elaborated at great length without containing a single affirma-tion or proposition because they are incapable of being tested by anything outside of themselves. They intersect with no other do-main of reality, whether empirical, religious, or even metaphysi-cal. Looked at in terms of their internal syntax, they may be in-tellectually exciting and perhaps even aesthetically rewarding, but they are semantically vacuous and therefore neither true nor false either in whole or part. Something similar would have to be said of theological systems and doctrinal statements when they have no clearly specifiable relation either negatively or pos-itively to the way Christians speak and act when actually living out their faith.

This does not mean that theological or doctrinal statements do not have propositional uses, do not make affirmations, but this chiefly happens when they function as part of the language of worship, preaching or action. The Nicean creed, for example, becomes an affirmation above all when it is used doxologically by the community or the individual to praise and glorify the Triune God.

The specifically dogmatic function of a doctrine is rather different, for in this it becomes a rule of language which dis-courages certain ways of expressing and inculcating the faith, and encourages others. Official formulations, as we have said, are second-order statements about the primary uses of the Christian tongue, and their properly dogmatic role is, not to affirm anything directly about God and his revelation, but to serve as directives which distinguish good and bad, correct and incorrect, safe and dangerous ways of speaking. In Wittgen-stein's metaphor, they articulate the rules of the game rather than being themselves part of the game.

Now they do this mostly in negative rather than positive ways. This is why it is so much easier to specify what a dogma denies than what it affirms. This is why it has been traditionally and quite rightly said that the meaning of a dogma can be more precisely determined from the canons where false views are anathematized, than from the chapters where doctrine is positively expounded. The positive exposition is necessarily extremely limited, because in order to discover the full significance of what Christians affirm about the Trinity, or Christ, or grace, or justification, one would have, in effect, to reproduce their entire language with its infinitely varied and nuanced ways of speaking about God's self-communication.

A more traditional way of making the same point is to say that the knowledge of faith infinitely surpasses that of intellect. More than that, the glory, majesty and mystery of God's revelation of himself vastly transcends anything human beings can say either on the primary level of use of the secondary level of theological reflection. We never adequately comprehend the positive meaning of any of our religious affirmations. Especially on the level of theological and doctrinal formulations, there is therefore always room for improvement and for new interpretations, some of which may be radically different from the old. Consequently it is only the negative meaning of dogmatic statements which can be specified with a relatively high degree of precision. We know very little positively about that divine Trinity which Nicea affirmed, but we can say that the council unequivocally excluded the Arian subordinationist affirmations about the relation of the Son to the Father. The same can be said of all doctrines because they all, insofar as they are affirmations of faith, point to the presence of the divine mystery. From this perspective, Roman Catholics also would want to say that they know very little positively about what is affirmed by the Immaculate Conception, or the Assumption, or even the infallibility of the Pope, but they can identify quite unambiguously certain affirmations which are excluded and certain ways of talking which are discouraged by these dogmas.

If, then, dogmatic definitions in their specifically dogmatic function are to be properly understood as chiefly negative language rules, we are in a position to ask in a new way whether those which have developed in the course of time are henceforth and forever essential to the integrity of the faith and therefore irreversibly dogmatic.

The question, it should be observed, is not traditional, and therefore there are no clear answers given in the tradition. It was assumed in the past by Protestants as well as Catholics that, providing the Church was right in saying a given belief is essential, then it would always remain essential. The difference between the two groups at this point was not on what we are calling dogmatic, but magisterial infallibility. The Reformers insisted that the Church and its teaching office might be wrong in identifying a given belief as essential, and that therefore every creed and confession must be constantly open to revision, or conceivably even repeal, on the basis of a better understanding of the Bible. This was what made the *sola scriptura* principle so important for them. But they, like their Roman Catholic brethren, did not raise the question of whether a doctrine which was in fact once essential, guaranteed by the totality of Christian faith and action as this had to be lived out in a particular situation, might cease to be so. We now, however, cannot avoid the question, for it has been raised by our much greater awareness of historical change and cultural and intellectual pluralism.

The standard Catholic answer, as we have already noted, is that this cannot happen. If an affirmation once becomes essential to the faith, it must always remain so. Dogmatic development is irreversible. Now, however, the possibility of at least some reversible developments is being recognized.

The doctrine of transubstantiation may be taken as an example. This, to be sure, is somewhat unsatisfactory because it is doubtful that it has ever been formally dogmatized. Trent says of the term simply that it is *"aptissime"* which seems to suggest that the doctrine is a highly appropriate way of speaking rather than a genuine affirmation of the kind which must be true or false. Nevertheless, it is an example of a doctrine which was once assumed to be fully dogmatic and which now even fairly conservative theologians suggest is perhaps only temporarily guaranteed by the Catholic language system. Expressed in our terminology, they say, in effect, that this doctrine was required by the central affirmations, and perhaps also the basic syntax, of the faith in answer to questions or problems which arose about Christ's eucharistic presence in a particular social, cultural, liturgical and intellectual setting. It was an unnecessary doctrine in the first centuries, and the situation of the Eastern Orthodox, happily for them, was such that they never needed it. But given the way Western eucharistic piety developed with its excessive concentration on the elements, and given an Aristotelian intellectual framework, it became a necessary and in this sense infallible rule of speech. It excluded certain ways of speaking which had become vehicles of heretical affirmations even though at other periods they had been used in an orthodox sense (e.g., by St. Augustine). Now, however, with the recovery of the communal dimension of the eucharist and with the development of more adequate ways of conceptualizing the eucharistic presence of Christ, transubstantiation is losing this quality of necessity. It is no longer essential to the full integrity of the faith, nor is it guaranteed by the totality of Christian thought and behavior as this needs to be worked out in our situation. In short, it is possible for at least some genuinely infallible doctrines to lose their infallibility.

The Protestant's inclination is to stop the analysis at this point. He needs to affirm the kind of temporary infallibility which we have just seen attributed by some scholars to transubstantiation, but he thinks that he needs no more. The biblical witness must be interpreted in ways which are both new and binding in order to fit new situations, for otherwise the authority of the Gospel becomes, in the medieval metaphor, a wax nose to be pushed in any direction, but none of these new propositions need necessarily continue to be essential or even helpful in all other future situations. This is true, not only of the early Church's Trinitarian and Christological affirmations, but even of the Reformation justification *sola fide*. That is not the *articulis stantis et cadentis ecclesiae* for, according to the Protestant biblical scholars themselves, it is not identical, though closely related, to the cognate affirmations of St. Paul. To be sure, it was necessary, it was essential, in the sixteenth century situation, but that is all that needs to be maintained. The position of the Reformers, stated in contemporary form, would perhaps be that temporary dogmatic infallibility—even though they of course did not call it that—suffices in order to do justice to the absoluteness of Christian claims.

We have spoken only of post-scriptural affirmations, but it

is important to observe that in the analysis we are employing, it
is at least possible that some biblical doctrinal affirmations may
also be at one time infallible—necessary to the integrity of the
Christian message—and then later cease to be. I am not thinking here of injunctions which are obviously relative to a specific
situation such as St. Paul's admonition to women to keep their
heads covered and remain silent in the church, but of propositions which have always been affirmed, or at least not denied,
by the great majority of Christians. The Virgin Birth would
serve as a good illustration, but let us consider the even more
critical example of the empty tomb. To be sure, it is not clear
that all early Christians knew about this particular part of the
resurrection story—St. Paul, for example, never mentions
it—but at least none of them as far as we knew ever denied it,
and its denial, even if not the failure to affirm, does indeed seem
fundamentally incompatible with the utterly realistic centrality
which the resurrection has in the Christian story. Maybe a genuinely bodily resurrection does not necessarily imply an empty
tomb—after all, we are told very little about glorified bodies
and their relation to mundane ones—but given the nature of the
Christian story and the way it talks about the power of God and
the final eschatological transformation of the universe, including
the earth, including its physicality, it generates considerable ten-
sions in the language system to deny the possibility that Christ's
tomb was empty, to deny that some kind of volatilization might
have occurred. To do that is to set up another language system,
the scientific one in which we learnedly talk about "the law of
the conservation of matter", as a dictator over what we can say
in the Christian one. And furthermore, we know no more in any
ultimate eschatological sense about the conservation of matter
than we do about glorified bodies. It seems, then, that as long as
earthly history continues it will be essentially or infallibly wrong
to deny the possibility that Christ's tomb was empty.

When looked at from this angle, it becomes difficult to
imagine that there ever will be a time when unapologetically
Christian communities will find themselves at ease with positive
assertions that the physical remains of Jesus remained in the
grave on Easter morning (though I can, for the reasons just out-

lined, imagine that they might be content with agnosticism on this point). Still, it is possible in principle to conceive of a change even on a matter like this, a change in situation which makes the denial of the empty tomb acceptable. As far as I know, there are no theological considerations of either a traditional or modern kind which try to rule out the possibility that the Christian community might again, sometime before the *eschaton,* have actual experience of resurrected, glorified human beings. If this were to happen, the Christian way of talking about them would be to say that they were in a sense more real, far more intensely charged with actuality, than in their pre-resurrection state, and their reality would also have to be called a bodily reality because it was so thoroughly concrete and fully human. But what if their graves and coffins were empty? At that point it would become clear, though probably not before, that it is consistent with Christian affirmations about the genuine, bodily resurrection of our Lord to say that his tomb was empty.

Now, to return to the main course of the discussion, if even biblical affirmations such as that of the empty tomb might conceivably lose their guaranteed or infallible character, then it seems foolhardy to suggest that there may be some doctrines which were not even explicitly known in the early Church and which yet much later in history acquire an irrevocable or irreversible infallibility. It would seem that all the later dogmas could lose their essential and therefore their guaranteed character. We have already mentioned this possibility, not only in reference to transubstantiation, but also to early Trinitarian and Christological affirmations. It it is true of such historically crucial affirmations, then it should be easy to add the Marian and papal dogmas to the list.

This, however, is not a decisive argument, as we shall see in a moment, but first it should be observed that rather less depends on this question of total reversibility than might at first be thought. We have already suggested that it is the position which Protestants might be expected to favor, because it appears to support a stronger version of the *sola scriptura* principle than would otherwise be possible. Even if infallible dogma is not limited to the Bible, and even if some biblical doctrines are perhaps

only temporarily necessary, still all irrevocably infallible affirmations of faith would, on this view, be limited to the Christological core found in Scripture. To be sure, even without this,
Scripture is *sola* in the sense of *norma normans non normata*
because it contains the most direct witnesses to the central revelatory events, but most Protestants would not be unhappy if
they could say more.

Perhaps even Catholics, however, need not be greatly dis-
turbed by the possibility that all post-biblical dogmas are reversible. This does not deny the present infallibility of any dogmas,
nor does it assert that they will in fact some day be reversed.
They may, even if in principle reversible, turn out to be *de facto*
permanent simply because the circumstances under which they
would no longer be necessary to the full integrity of the faith are
never actualized. It is hard to see why this view should be considered incompatible with the maintenence of full Roman Catholic identity. The Roman communion could still be considered
the one true Church in the sense that it alone has all the institutional means Christ wills for his Church. It could still be
affirmed as that Christian body in which the Church of Christ
most fully subsists; and while it would be admitted that there is
no absolute necessity that it always remain so, one could still
hopefully trust for the very sake of the Gospel that God in his
mercy would never allow it to lapse from that high and responsible estate. Such a position would meet the Protestant objections to Catholic "ecclesiolatry", and as I shall further suggest in
discussing magisterial infallibility, it is not clear that it is logically inconsistent with Roman, and even rather conservative
Roman, orthodoxy.

Nevertheless, while the reversibility of all dogmatic developments may be compatible with orthodoxy, there are difficulties in granting that it is true. Is the condemnation of slavery reversible? Isn't the Church forever committed to this, even
though it is a biblical development? Is it really possible that circumstances could again arise when Christians would feel under
no obligation to disapprove of slavery as a social institution?
Protestants as well as Catholics are reluctant to answer "yes" to
any of these questions, thus suggesting that they in fact, what-

ever their theory might be, regard the condemnation of slavery as an irreversibly infallible development. Unlike the early Christians, we now know that it is possible within sinful human history to have societies without institutionalized chattel slavery. As soon as Christians know that this is a possibility, the way they talk about the love of God and man obligates them, if they take it seriously, to disapprove of any slave-holding social order and to seek to change it. Further, this insight into the possibility of slaveless societies seems most unlikely to disappear. Total forgetfulness on this point would seem to require a historical discontinuity so drastic that the very memories of Jesus Christ which are the life-blood of the Church would also disappear. And that, so the Christian language system asserts implicitly and explicitly in many ways, can never happen. Here then would seem to be an instance of a doctrinal development which seems irreversibly infallible. Oddly enough, it is often bitterly anti-dogmatic liberals who are most likely to insist on this.

The general principle at work is easy enough to identify. Even bitter opponents of optimistic progress theories have to admit that both natural and historical processes have a certain cumulative character. The cosmos evolves and so do plants and animals, and when human beings emerge, a new kind of cumulation begins. To use Bernard Lonergan's terminology, insights accumulate more and more in different areas, and from time to time there is a breakthrough to a new level, a higher viewpoint, a broader outlook, in which not only new questions, but new kinds of questions are raised, and must be given new kinds of answers.[9] For example, as we have just seen, the Christian community is confronted, not only with the New Testament question of how to act in old and new circumstances toward the slaves who are Christian and human brothers, but with the further and broader question of how to evaluate institutions and the social orders of which they are a part. The Christian answer to such a new question can be just as irreversible as to an old one.

Besides slavery, there are perhaps other examples of irreversible developments in the field of social ethics. Monogamy, not only for bishops as in the New Testament, but for all Christians, would be a candidate, and I personally hope that full and genuine equality for women in Church and society will soon become one. In other areas of doctrine, however, it is hard to think of persuasive examples.

The Trinitarian and Christological definitions of Nicea and Chalcedon would seem to be much the best possibilities, providing one interprets them as Lonergan does,[10] viz., as rules for correct Christian linguistic usage. He agrees with Augustine that *"persona* or *substantia* was an undefined heuristic concept" saying no more than that "as long as the Trinity is acknowledged, there are acknowledged three of something". In reference to Christology, he asks (I shall paraphrase): Do you grant that some things should be said of Jesus Christ which can be said truly only of God, and others which can be said only of one who is truly man? If so, you acknowledge the two natures. Do you accept that these two sets of statements refer to *one and the same Jesus Christ*? If so, you acknowledge what is meant by one hypostasis. This may well be, not a modern distortion of what the authors of these conciliar decrees had in mind, but rather exactly what they consciously wanted to affirm. Athanasius himself, we recall, viewed the whole of the Trinitarian decree as being expressed in the formula, "eadem de Filio quae de Patre dicuntur, excepto Patris nomine." So understood, these early dogmas are a development analogous to the technical formulations of the basic syntax of a natural language. They are a movement to a higher viewpoint, to a second-level of technical language about the primary language, and as long as the primary language remains the same language, as long as Christian speech remains recognizably Christian, these rules state the way to speak the language in order to avoid what within it is nonsense. Contrary, then, to the Protestant interpretation which I mentioned earlier, they are irrevocably binding.

Outside of these few examples, however, it is difficult to think of plausible cases of irreversibility. Other developments might in fact be permanent or even irreversible, but if so, the reasons are difficult to articulate. In reference to specifically Roman Catholic dogmas, for example, it might be argued that papal primacy has been essential to the welfare of the Church under the circumstances which have prevailed through most of Christian history. It has made the Church far more independent of the state and also more flexible than in the East where, because of magisterial weakness, a static, though often admirable traditionalism has been combined with Caesaro-papism. At the same time, Roman adaptability has not been purchased at the cost of the fragmentation and discontinuities (and, in the case of Lutheranism and Anglicanism, also Caesaro-papism) which have plagued Protestantism. Looked at in sociological and historical terms, Christianity, including non-Catholic Christianity, might not have survived to anywhere near the present extent if it were not for the massive bulk, international spread, relative adaptability and unity and continuity of Roman Catholicism, and it is in large part because of the papacy that this difficult combination has been possible. Yet it would be hard to show on such empirical-prudential grounds that the papal office will always be indispensable or even helpful. Perhaps the world will, or already has, changed so much that the same values will be better promoted by other means. The Marian dogmas represent a similar case. A Catholic could argue that they have served a vital function within the Church's life and the Christian language system, at least in its Roman Catholic version, but it is difficult to see how one would go about constructing a case that this must always be so.

Yet this reasoning is not decisive. As is true of reality itself, there are far more things in a language than has been dreamed of in any philosophy or theology. Involved in the way we speak, are complex syntactical structures too subtle for reflective reason to grasp, yet easy for the child to use, and so tenacious that they dictate the limits of the ways in which philosophers and poets and everyone in between can perceive and conceive the world. Further, like English, the Christian language grows and changes. It acquires Greek and Latin, French and German, and innumerable other elements which enable it to express both new and old truths in endlessly varying ways. It may become essential, in order to speak the language well, to talk about some matters in quite a different way than was previously appropriate. And it is the skilled speakers of the language, the poets and proclaimers of the religious life, not its theological and philosophical grammarians and logicians, who discover what these new ways are. Some of these developments may be irreversible, and the grammarians and logicians may never be able to discover why. It is such considerations which make it impossible to say of any dogma, whether this be papal, Marian or eucharistic, that it is reversible until the course of history does in fact reverse it. This happens when it no longer plays a critically helpful role in maintaining a faith and life centered on Jesus Christ.

There are objective tests which can be applied. Within Christianity, any development which cannot be made to express or sustain the central Christological affirmations and the forms of life in which they are embedded is clearly suspect. Yet however critical one may be of the various guises assumed by Marian or papal doctrine in the past, it is hard to be sure, especially in these days of proposed reforms, that they will never take an authentically Christic shape, and to the extent that this happens, their possible irreversibility must be left an open question. Much the same would have to be said about various Protestant developments such as the sixteenth-century version of the *sola fide* and Protestant individualism and biblicism. To the extent that they become expressions and supports for the *sola Christi*, their legitimate permanence becomes a possibility.

Catholics and Protestants are likely to continue to differ on these points, however, for though they share a common Christian language, they speak different dialects of it. What is appropriate or essential in one dialect is not in the other. To be sure, there are ways of carrying on arguments and dialogues across linguistic boundaries even when these mark chasms between different ways of living the Christian life; but these are rather like discussions between the English and the Americans as to which of their two versions of the same language is superior, with the English including post-seventeenth-century English usage and the Americans post-seventeenth American usage in their respective normative traditions, while both agree that Shakespearian and pre-Shakespearian literature is canonical.

Thus we see that the approach we are following does not

provide any neat way of settling theological controversies once for all. It is, I would suppose, confessionally neutral, and can be used by the Orthodox, Catholics or Protestants for their particular purposes. Its virtue, if it has any, is that it offers a more adequate conceptuality, strips away irrelevancies, and helps identify the real issues.

These issues in the infallibility debate, according to what has so far been said, are not whether there are infallibly guaranteed affirmations: there clearly are within a Christian context. Nor is the question whether some dogmatic developments are irreversible: some perhaps are, some clearly are not, and it perhaps makes no crucial difference either way. The fundamental problem is one which we have not yet discussed—that of magisterial infallibility—and it is to this that we must now turn.

III. Magisterial Infallibility and Vatican I

Given a contextual and functional approach to the problem of meaning such as we have been employing, the question of the significance of the doctrine of infallibility can be divided into three parts. What would such a doctrine mean in terms of the analysis of the nature of dogma which we have proposed? What did it mean in the context of Vatican I? And what, thirdly, is the import of the affirmations made at Vatican I in the present situation of the Church?

In this discussion we shall abstract both from the question of the papacy and from historical inquiry. The basic problems are the same for our particular purposes no matter what authority is declared infallible—whether pope, council or the Executive Committee of the World Council of Churches. Further, if our rather conventional assumptions [11] about what infallibility meant to the bishops at Vatican I are wrong, this analysis would have to be revised, but the same basic procedure might still prove useful.

As is true of most contemporary approaches to magisterial authority, the one we are employing suggests that the teaching office is justified in making dogmatic pronouncements only in the most extreme circumstances. Such pronouncements involve ex-communication, and given the essential character of the Church as a community of love, excommunication is a last resort. Dog-matic definition is perhaps allowable only when there is a con-troversy over a previously undecided question which threatens to rend the unity of the Church or destroy its integrity. Then, when all discussion and pastoral and disciplinary measures fail, it may be necessary to make a definitive decision binding on all those who wish to remain in communion. This is what happened in the Trinitarian and Christological disputes of the early Church, the Reformation debates, and perhaps also in the crisis which climaxed at Barmen. There may have been other occa-sions which legitimated the formulation of "new dogma", but they have not been numerous.

The reasons for this reticence are in part, as we have seen, that the determination of what is truly essential to the life of faith occurs fundamentally on levels which are only partially and un-certainly accessible to theological reason and even less accessi-ble to the clumsy fiats of juridically constituted authorities. Further, even the best and most necessary of dogmatic decisions is a risky business with evil as well as good consequences: it breaks off communication, is inevitably unjust to some of those involved in the controversy, and restricts the area of free dis-cussion in the Church. In traditional terminology, lack of love and prudence may make a formally correct decision into a very bad dogma which harms the Church more than would have been done by not so sharply excluding the error against which it was directed. Only if the dogmatic decision is prudent and charitable is it justified.

From this point of view, a strong doctrine of magisterial infallibility would hold that the teaching office is preserved from the error of making unjustified doctrinal decisions, viz., those which do more harm than good to the Church.

No ecclesiastical body has ever formally claimed for itself anything remotely resembling this degree of infallibility (though in practice a great many of them seem to do so). Certainly the doctrine of Vatican I is much weaker. All that it claims is that the magisterium in defining doctrine is preserved from the error

of promulgating a falsehood. The act of defining may be impru-
dent and uncharitable and the final doctrinal formulation may
be highly inadequate, confused and even dangerously misleading.
The one thing of which one can be sure is that it is not a false
proposition.

This, however, is a remarkably modest claim from the point
of view which we have adopted. Not only may a "not false" doctrinal statement be a very bad dogma, but it may not even be
true. It may, in other words, not be a proposition or affirmation
at all. It may not express a judgment which is capable of being
either true or false, but may rather, as we have suggested, state
a rule for the use of language (or conceivably be meaningless
in the strong sense of failing even to do that—but this is a possibility we shall not discuss). Vatican I does not exclude the
possibility of absolutely disastrous linguistic rules, but only of
propositions which are "not false". A good many Protestants,
and apparently some Catholics also, would analyze many of the
decrees of the Council of Trent in these terms. They are not
false, but they are also, in both intention and effect, dangerously
erroneous directives which have badly misled the Catholic
Church in the last four hundred years of its development. As
an historical judgment, that may well be unbalanced and unfair,
but at any rate, it seems to be compatible with the doctrine of
infallibility enunciated at Vatican I. That doctrine, whatever the
intentions of the authors, apparently does not exclude the most
serious errors which can infect the dogmatizing process. The
bishops perhaps wanted to say more than they did, but they
failed. Like legislators who frame laws which are immediately
riddled with loopholes by sharp-shooting lawyers, the bishops
simply did not consider all the questions and problems which
need to be covered.

Perhaps rationalism is the cause of their failure, because it
is characteristically rationalistic to divide the world into the
propositionally true and false, to suppose that nothing is important except what can be judged by the intellect in *actus
secundus,* and therefore to imagine that, apart from obvious ex-
ceptions, all sentences which have the grammatical form of
propositions actually express propositions. Most utterances,

however, even when the mood is indicative, function in other ways. "The room is cold" frequently means "Close the window." What look like affirmations may be imperatives, expressions of attitudes, feelings, praise, blame, stipulations of meaning, explanations, indications of syntactical connections, and numberless other things. Perhaps especially in theoretical discourse, genuine judgments are rare. Scientists often find it necessary to spend thousands of words in elaborating highly complex and precise theories before they can make a single affirmation—e.g., a prediction. Similarly, theologians may engage in vast intellectual labors before they get clear enough on what they mean and what is the relevant evidence to enunciate a conscious and deliberate proposition. Now the councils of the Church have not been totally unaware of this, and so their discussions have generally been protracted; but still the problems of making a meaningful assertion—an assertion which can be true or false—are, we now see, much greater than they thought, and that is why they often made syntactical recommendations lacking direct semantic reference when they thought they were formulating propositions. But a dogma which is a recommendation for the religious uses of language is good or bad, not true or false, and so is not covered by what Vatican I says about infallibility.

To be sure, there are some dogmas which do seem clearly to enunciate propositions, and so it might be wise to examine one of these more closely to see in what sense it actually succeeds. The doctrine of the Assumption provides a particularly apt test case because it clearly does not simply say that such and such is a good and fruitful way to talk about the Virgin (or about grace, sin or faith), but affirms that a particular event took place.

Yet it is doubtful that even this is really a proposition. Technically expressed, it is more like a propositional form than a propositional function. What I mean by this is that a form of words such as "Socrates sits" does not, apart from a concrete context in which words are actually being used to do things, make an affirmation. Rather, it delimits a wide, though finite, range of possible propositions. Before it can function proposi-

tionally, a precise place, time and person must be specified, and
this might take pages of exposition for someone unfamiliar with
our history and our geography. In a partially similar way, the
dogma of the Assumption specifies a range of possible affirmations—or in the perhaps less exact language of Continental
hermeneutics, "interpretations"—but does not itself affirm any
one of them.

One such possible affirmation, for example, can be devised
by combining Karl Rahner's treatment of the Assumption with
his theory of the "world relation" of the dead,[12] and might be
stated thus: Mary now bodily participates more fully than most—
but not necessarily all—the redeemed in Christ's resurrection,
even though all believers who have departed this life also already share in it to some extent. It would seem that the dogma
does not necessarily affirm more than this, and so interpreted,
it appears harmless and perhaps even acceptable, from a Protestant perspective. Consider, however, what happens on the level
of the primary uses of religious language where alone, so we
have earlier suggested, doctrines become affirmations which can
be adjudged true or false in a religiously significant way. When
actually used in the concrete context of traditional Marian piety,
the dogma of the Assumption is filled with a far different, much
stronger and, to most Protestants, abhorrent propositional
content. Presumably this is what the propounder of the dogma,
Pius XI, did with it in his own devotions.

Yet one could perhaps agree with this Protestant assessment
of the traditional propositional content of the dogma and yet not
contradict the view of Vatican I that *qua* dogma it is infallibly
true. A propositional form is not false providing at least one of
its possible propositional functions (or "interpretations") is true.
It is not false even if its original framers were unaware of the
sense in which it can be true and themselves made it into a
false affirmation when they actually used it rather than simply
defining it.

In conclusion, then, it would seem that the doctrine of infallibility as defined at Vatican I affirms only that a dogmatic
proposition is never so hopelessly false that it is incapable of
being given a true interpretation. Even the question of whether

it will ever be given a true interpretation is left open. It postulates a certain immunity from falsehood on the theoretical level, but not on the primary level where a dogma becomes a genuine affirmation. In short, it would seem that Vatican I succeeded in affirming only what would normally be considered a form of magisterial indefectibility: the teaching office will always be sufficiently sustained in the truth so that there will be the possibility of its correcting its errors.

In addition to what it says on infallibility, however, Vatican I asserts that a dogmatic definition is "irreformable" and that its own doctrine of infallibility is "revealed". "Irreformability" functions in the decree as equivalent to "unappealability" [13]—there is no appeal from a papal dogmatic decision to Church or council; but in its more general meaning it seems simply to say that a dogma is indeed, like any other truth, forever true. One of the formulations proposed at Vatican I, for example, says that the pope defines infallibly "so that his decrees are irreformable, i.e., immune from all error" (*ut irreformabilia id est ab omni errore immunia, sint eius decreta*).[14] Thus the notion of infallibility apparently adds nothing materially to infallibility, but simply makes the purely formal point that what is infallibly (not falsely) said is itself not false. In any case, it is quite clear from the discussions surrounding the decree that its authors quite consciously did not want to say that the verbal or conceptual formulation of a definition is "irreformable", but only that the underlying affirmation is.

As to the revealed character of the dogma, it is at this point that the always difficult logical problems of self-referential statements become most acute. The doctrine of infallibility has the logically unique status among dogmas of being a third-order statement, for it is not a second-order statement about the primary uses of religious language, but is itself about all second-order statements, and then also about at least one third-order statement, viz., itself. The logical problems discussed in the theory of types are therefore relevant, but it is particularly when revelation enters the picture, and not simply infallibility and irreformability, that these become more than a logical puzzle.

The function of the reference to revelation is presumably

similar to the fuller reference one finds in such a definition as that of the Immaculate Conception: this is "revealed by God and therefore to be firmly and steadfastly believed by all the faithful".[15] It would seem, then, that the purpose of explicitly mentioning the revealed character of the dogma in this context is to affirm that it has the specifically dogmatic property of being, in the terminology we have been using, "essential to the integrity of the faith".

But it was not always essential, at least not as an explicitly articulated and formally promulgated doctrine. Might it then perhaps some day cease to be essential? The bishops at Vatican I would no doubt be shocked at the suggestion, but at the same time, they never discussed the question; and if it is impossible to answer an unasked question, this means that the possibility of reversibility has been left open. Perhaps someday, perhaps now, it will become unnecessary to talk the language of magisterial infallibility. It would seem that the dogma of infallibility does not exclude its own demise, and consequently it is compatible with a doctrine of the defectibility or reversibility of the Roman Catholic status as in some sense the one true Church (for if the Roman magisterium became radically defectible, it might promulgate falsehoods which would destroy this character of the Roman Catholic Church). Thus perhaps even infallibility does not foreclose the possibility of the kind of Roman Catholic orthodoxy which, as we suggested earlier, would continue to insist on the special status of Roman Catholicism as the Christian communion in which the Church of Christ most fully subsists, but which would have surrendered the pretension of claiming that it must be irreversibly so.

There is no point, however, in further discussing this speculative and extremely weak interpretation of the doctrine. With the possible exception of Hans Küng, it seems that no serious Catholic theologian has so far proposed it.

What has been proposed, however, is that somewhat stronger version of the doctrine, which makes it equivalent to magisterial indefectibility, for which we have already argued. All I have done is offer a kind of linguistic analytic case for the impossibility of making the dogma say more than what Karl

Rahner, who is currently intent on defending the dogma, has already insisted on theological grounds is its proper interpretation.

He says that magisterial indefectibility (which he agrees is one and the same thing as infallibility) would be violated only "if the highest teaching and pastoral office of the Church were to make use of its highest teaching and pastoral authority over the whole Church with a force definitively binding upon all with fullest obligation, and in doing so were to contradict the truth and the salvific will of Christ to such an extent that the acceptance and following of such an act would place the universal Church as a whole in unambiguous contradiction to Christ, and so into absolute error as 'No' to his truth or as 'No' to his unifying and sanctifying love".[16]

As far as I can see, even a fanatical anti-Catholic might hesitate to claim that the Roman Church has ever erred this drastically (even though, of course, he would differ from the Catholic by insisting it *could* so err). Anyone with a modicum of charity and fairness would find it hard to argue that even the Marian or papal dogmas are "absolute error" in the sense of placing the Roman communion as a whole in "unambiguous contradiction to Christ". If this is all that infallibility excludes, then it would be quite possible to combine a firm rejection of all the specifically Roman dogmas as at present interpreted with the view that the Roman Church has not yet proved itself fallible and with the hope, even if not belief, that it will never do so.

Actually it is doubtful that Rahner (though not Küng, and perhaps not Kasper) intends to be as minimalistic as this quotation, taken in isolation, seems to imply, but still he clearly has a most modest view of what infallibility involves. The grounds for this need explanation. It is not the result of the contextual linguistic considerations we have advanced, but is a quasi-logical necessity from his own more traditional theological perspective.

The notion of doctrinal infallibility simply cannot be given any coherent sense unless it is interpreted very restrictively. This is true if one acknowledges, as even conservative theologians must, that dogmatic formulations are of necessity radically perfectible (which, of course, means that they are also radically deficient) expressions of divine truth. "Now we see in a glass darkly, then face to face." The knowledge of the *viator* is dim indeed in comparison to the glory which shall be revealed. Human concepts and language are by their very nature thoroughly inadequate media for the enunciation of revelation. That is why Aquinas insisted that all our talk of God and his actions must be analogous—not quite equivocal, but still far from unequivocal or unambiguous. These traditional emphases are, of course, greatly intensified by the contemporary awareness of the way in which the meanings of all doctrinal statements are conditioned and limited by the historical, cultural and practical situations in which they are formulated. This is a lesser problem in reference to much of the "ordinary religious language" of worship or of the biblical stories. The parable of the Good Samaritan, for example, or stories of a man who died and rose again, are readily intelligible, even if not believable, to both cave men and space men. But the more technical theological language in which dogmas are inevitably couched (for they are interpretations of the ordinary language statements) are peculiarly subject to obsolescence.

In the very nature of the case, therefore, doctrinal formulations can be "without error" in only a highly limited sense. They are sufficiently exempt from error so that they need never be so changed that they affirm what they explicitly deny or deny what they explicitly affirm.

They can, however, be reinterpreted in an indefinite variety of ways, or be supplemented by statements which are more adequate to revelation or to new situations. It is possible, also, therefore, that they may in practice be replaced: a more adequate formulation may supplant less adequate ones as Nicea, for example, supplanted older Christological creeds which were in their day orthodox but had become susceptible to heretical interpretation. It is conceivable that the reverse process could also occur: an originally objectionable statement could lose its heretical connotations in a new situation (cf. the widespread contemporary Catholic view of the Reformation *sola fide*). The one thing that cannot happen to an infallible dogma is that it be from all perspectives and in all situations false—i.e., irreconcilable with revealed truth, i.e., incapable of being given an interpretation consistent with the Gospel.

This brings us to a final problem which falls outside the limits of the present discussion, but is really of central importance. What is the function of infallibility? On the basis of the analysis we have presented, it is of no positive help to the teaching office. Its role is essentially negative, and even then so limited as to be of questionable usefulness. An infallible magisterium does not necessarily teach the right things, but is simply guaranteed against major errors, against binding the Church to what is flatly and irremediably false. It does not insure the presence of the positive power of effectively proclaiming the Word of God. The fullest manifestations of that power are almost always found, not in infallible councils or popes, but in non-infallible lay and clerical teachers, preachers, prophets and professors. It is they who chiefly mediate the living Word which sustains and nourishes God's people and provides them with vitality and strength. It is also they who, in combination with the *sensus fidelium* (so Cardinal Newman would argue), are the chief bastions against heresy. St. Augustine (and St. Thomas too, for that matter) have done more to oppose Pelagianism and semi-Pelagianism within the Roman ranks than all popes and councils together. A Church endowed with the negative gift of infallibility in its official dogma, but lacking the positive teaching charisms, would not only be starved and sterile, but also riddled with heresies in its ordinary life and teaching. Why, then, bother with infallibility? Why claim that an official dogma, however inadequate, or even false as ordinarily understood, is not irremediably false? The early Church, after all, made no such claims and seemed to manage considerably better than some of its infallibilist successors.

Once the question is posed this way, the answer is obvious. Infallibility functions, not so much to insure correct and effective teaching and preaching, but to help maintain the unity of the Church. There must be a final assembly or court of appeal to decide disputes which cannot be settled in any other way and which threaten to rend the Church. This is true either formally or informally in any organized community which values visible unity, whether the community be religious or secular, Protestant or Catholic. But if this unity is in addition regarded as an ultimate value, an irrevocable gift of God whose loss is unthinkable, then, in a Christian context, the final adjudicator of controversies must be infallible, must be divinely protected against final error, even if not against preliminary falsity.

This is necessary because otherwise believers would sometimes not be able in good conscience to remain in the Church when it decided against them. They could not be confident that they were not thereby violating their primary loyalty to Jesus Christ. They would not be able to trust that, whatever the deficiencies of a given decision, it was still; even though they might not be able to see this, reconcilable with the Gospel.[17]

Clearly such a position depends, as we have already said, on a high estimate of the importance of the Church's visible unity. It involves the conviction that God wills unity, not only "wishfully" or "eschatologically", but with present and enduring efficacity. That is, he wills that there always be a specific ecclesiastical community from which, because it is preserved from absolute error, it is never objectively necessary or obligatory for the believer to separate himself. (It may, to be sure, be *subjectively* necessary or even objectively *permissible* for him to do so, but that is another question.)

This would seem to be the fundamental issue raised by the Roman Catholic (and Orthodox) doctrine of infallibility. Does or does not God efficaciously will enduring visible unity for his Church? If he does, then there is a basis even from a Reformation viewpoint for affirming magisterial infallibility or indefectibility of the limited kind we have described to some office within the Church (though fully ecumenical councils would seem to be better candidates for this role than are popes).[18] If not, there is no such basis.

If there is any merit to this analysis, then it becomes at least imaginable that good Catholics and good Protestants, loyal sons of their respective traditions, might some day reach agreement on a refined and revised interpretation of infallibility. It would be a mistake, however, to greet this prospect, even if it were near and vivid, with any great enthusiasm. Infallibility is becoming a dead letter. This is the final conclusion to emerge from this discussion.

The reason for saying this is that, if we are right, magisterial infallibility is important only as an aid in maintaining unity. But it now plays this role less and less effectively even in the Roman communion.[19] In our new historical situation, schism over dogmatic issues is becoming less and less likely. In part this is the result of an anti-institutionalism which involves disillusionment with the possibility of ever finding or founding a Church better than the one in which one already finds oneself. The dissident isn't tempted to start another ecclesiastical establishment. Rather he stays and fights, or goes underground, or drops out. Further, official teachings, whether fallible or infallible, are losing their authority. Neither those who agree nor those who disagree take them with the old seriousness. Consequently, heretics don't feel conscience-bound to leave the Church and the orthodox are not particularly intent on driving them out.

Perhaps doctrinal infallibility could be functional only during the "Constantinian" era from which we are now emerging when there were powerful social and legal pressures to keep men within the Church and when there were non-religious means of enforcing conformity to juridically formulated standards of correct belief. As these factors disappear, the authoritativeness of the Church's teachings and decisions comes to depend more and more on their intrinsic power and persuasiveness. The avoidance of infallible dogmatic definitions at Vatican II reflects some awareness of this. Designating a given teaching as "infallible" would not guarantee that it be listened to. The Churches must learn once again to rely for unity in the faith, as in the early centuries, on the positive power of God's Spirit and Word, not on the pallid gift of lack of contradiction to revelation.

NOTES

1. Hans Küng, *Infallible? An Inquiry* (Doubleday, 1971) p. 170.
2. *Ibid.*, p. 179.
3. *Ibid.*, p. 183.

4. Reprinted in *Herder Korrespondenz*, March, 1971, p. 156.

5. For example, Rahner argues that the Church's doctrinal decisions must be infallible at least in the sense of not falling into the error of rejecting what is fundamental to the faith, for otherwise she would not be indefectible. See "Replik," *Stimmen der Zeit* 187 (1971) p. 151.

6. Needless to say, there is nothing original about this criticism. Xavier Charpe comments that Küng's failure to distinguish between what he, writing in French, calls the "judgment" and the "propositions" through which it is expressed has been a favorite point of attack. *Informations Catholiques Internationales* (April 1, 1971) p. 29.

7. *Language, Thought and Reality, Selected Writings of Benjamin Lee Whorf*, ed. John B. Carroll (Massachusetts Institute of Technology, 1956) contains four papers related to this theme. This and similar views have been subjected to a good critical analysis by Paul Henle in a book he edited, *Language, Thought and Culture* (University of Michigan Press, 1966) pp. 1-24.

8. *Summa Theologica* II-II, q. 2, a. 3, ad 3.

9. *Insight* (London: Longmans, Green & Co., revised edition, 1958). See especially the sections on development, pp. 451-487.

10. All the material in this paragraph is taken from "The Dehellenization of Dogma," *Theological Studies* (Vol. 28, 1967) pp. 336-351, esp. pp. 344-347.

11. These assumptions are those of many, perhaps most, competent scholars as represented, for example by Yves Congar, "Infaillibilite et Indefectibilite," *Revue des Sciences Philosophiques et Theologiques* (Vol. 54, 1970) pp. 601-618.

12. See Rahner's treatment of the Assumption in *Theological Investigations*, Vol. I (Baltimore: Helicon, 1961) pp. 215-227; and his *Theology of Death* (New York: Herder & Herder, 1965), esp. pp. 16-26.

13. It will be recalled that the decree says that because the magisterium exercises the infallibility with which Christ wills to endow his Church, "therefore such definitions of the Roman Pontiff are irreformable of themselves, not however from the consent of the Church." Denzinger-Schönmetzer, 3074.

14. Cited by Congar, *op. cit.*, p. 607, fn. 22.

15. Denzinger-Schönmetzer, 2803.

16. *Theological Investigations*, Vol. VI (Baltimore: Helicon, 1970) p. 308. Rahner does not wish to be as minimalistic as this quotation, taken in isolation, seems to imply; but, nevertheless, it does express the reason why he thinks a doctrine of magisterial infallibility is indispensable. See also the reference in footnote 5 *supra*.

17. The use of the doctrine of magisterial infallibility to support this attitude—viz., an attitude which, while allowing for opposition to the magisterium, insists that this is "loyal"—seems to be the only possible legitimate function which the doctrine could have from a Reformation perspective.

18. This statement supposes that it is not necessary from a Reformation perspective to deny that the "undivided Church"—even if not the Roman portion of it taken in isolation—may be infallible in the specific sense of being preserved from fundamental dogmatic error. It would probably be impossible to find grounds in the writings of the Reformers for even so circumspect a doctrine of magisterial infallibility, but my own view is that it is not necessarily incompatible with the fundamental thrust of their thought. Further, for reasons which fall outside the scope of this paper, it is possible to argue that this could be sufficient for unity even from a genuinely Roman Catholic point of view.

19. Karl Rahner has pointed out that in the contemporary situation, when it is Christian belief in its totality which is questioned, the authority of the magisterium is even more suspect than are the central truths of the faith (for unless one accepts these beliefs, one will have no grounds for trusting the magisterium). Thus the teaching office must strive to present the central affirmations in such a way that they are intrinsically persuasive, and its own authority is rendered "superfluous". *Schriften zur Theologie*, Vol. IX (Einsiedeln: Benzinger, 1970) pp. 363-364.

Contributors

GREGORY G. BAUM

Gregory Baum is presently Professor of Theology at St. Michael's College, University of Toronto, editor of *The Ecumenist* and Associate Editor of *Journal of Ecumenical Studies.*

He is the author of numerous journal articles and several books: *That They May Be One* (1958), *The Jews and the Gospel* (1961), *Catholic Quest for Christian Unity* (1965), *Ecumenical Theology Today* (1965), *Ecumenical Theology No. 2* (1967), *Credibility of the Church Today* (1968), *Faith and Doctrine* (1969), *Man Becoming* (1970).

RICHARD P. McBRIEN

Richard P. McBrien is Associate Professor of Theology at Boston College and Visiting Professor of Theology at Pope John XXIII National Seminary in Weston, Massachusetts, where he formerly served for five years on the full-time faculty and for two years as the seminary's Dean of Studies.

He has published four books, *The Church in the Thought of Bishop John Robinson*, which has been translated into French and Spanish, *Do We Need the Church?*, *What Do We*

Really Believe?, and, most recently, *Church: The Continuing Quest.*

HARRY J. McSORLEY

Harry J. McSorley is presently a member of the theology faculty at St. Michael's College, University of Toronto, and lectures widely in the field of ecumenical studies and Lutheran theology and history.

He has studied under both Hans Küng and Karl Rahner and is the author of *Luther: Right or Wrong, An Ecumenical-Theological Study of Luther's Major Work, The Bondage of the Will* (1968). He has also published widely in journals.

GEORGE A. LINDBECK

George A. Lindbeck is Professor of Theology and Director of Graduate Studies, Department of Religious Studies, Yale University. He was a Delegated Observer from the Lutheran World Federation to the Second Vatican Council and among other assignments has been Research Professor of the Lutheran Foundation for Ecumenical Research (Strasbourg, France) and has taught as a visiting professor at Boston College and Trinity Theological College, Singapore.

He has published numerous articles, especially on medieval theology and contemporary Roman Catholicism, in a variety of periodicals and books; most recently, he has been editor and joint author of *Dialogue on the Way:* Protestants Report from Rome on Vatican Council (1965); and author of *The Future of Roman Catholic Theology* (1969).